WEST VIRGINIA

WEST VIRGINIA BY ROAD

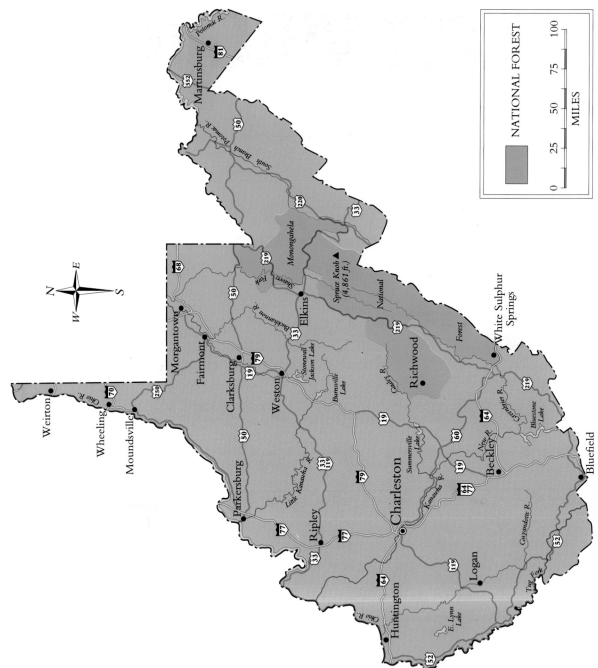

CELEBRATE THE STATES
WEST VIRGINIA

Nancy Hoffman

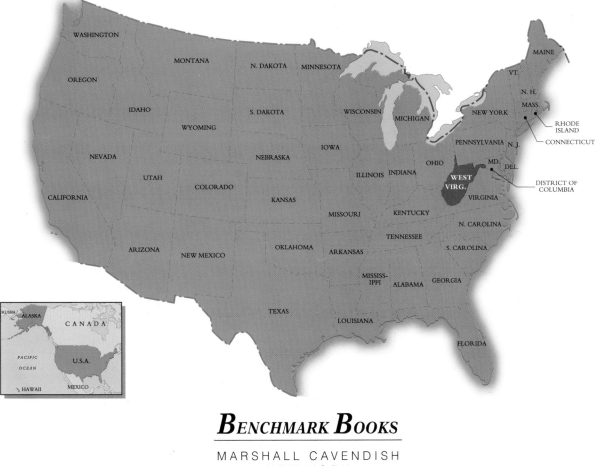

BENCHMARK BOOKS

MARSHALL CAVENDISH
NEW YORK

Benchmark Books
Marshall Cavendish Corporation
99 White Plains Road
Tarrytown, New York 10591-9001

Library of Congress Cataloging-in-Publication Data
Hoffman, Nancy, date.
West Virginia / Nancy Hoffman.
p.   cm. — (Celebrate the states)
Includes bibliographical references and index.
Summary: Relates the history and describes the geographic features, places of interest, government,
industry, environmental concerns, and life of the people of this largely rural state.
ISBN 0-7614-0665-4 (lib. bdg.)
1. West Virginia—Juvenile literature. [1. West Virginia.] I. Title. II. Series.
F241.3.H64   1999   975.4—dc21   97-32927   CIP   AC

Maps and graphics supplied by Oxford Cartographers, Oxford, England

Photo research by Ellen Barrett Dudley and Matthew J. Dudley

Cover photo: Richard Nowitz

The photographs in this book are used by permission and through the courtesy of: *West Virginia Division of
Tourism*: Steve Shaluta Jr., 6-7, 18, 21, 61, 80, 101, 107, 109, 123; David Fattaleh, 110-111. *Photo
Researchers, Inc.*: Jeff Greenberg, 10-11; Richard Nowitz, 15; Mark Newman, 24(left); Phil A. Dotson, 25;
Theodore Vogel-Rapho, 27, 62, 122; Ray Ellis, 54-55; Jeff Lepore, 103, 115(right); Jack Sullivan/Science
Source, 112; Stephen Krasemann, 115(left); Stephan Dalton, 119; Frederica Georgia, 133; *Richard Nowitz*: 15,
60, 68-69, 96-97, 99, backcover. *Eilene Moore*: 16, 17, 24(right), 72, 110, 111. *Permanent Art Collection, West
Virginia University Libraries*: 28-29. *Boston Public Library, Print Department*: 32. *Library of Congress LC-USZ62-
60816*: 35. *From the Collection of Oglebay Institute, Mansion Museum*: 37. *West Virginia State Archives*: 38, 43;
Boyd B. Stutler Collection, 40(top); Mary Behner Christopher Collection, 51. *Harpers Ferry National Historical
Park HF222*: 40(bottom). *West Virginia and Regional History Collection, West Virginia University Libraries*: 50.
AP/Wide World Photos: 52. *Steven Wayne Rotsch*: 64. *Stephen Shaluta Jr.*: 75, 76, 118. *Augusta Heritage Center*:
78, 79, 82- 83. *Corbis-Bettmann*: 85, 92, 127, 129(top & bottom), 130, 131(top). *UPI/Corbis-Bettmann*: 86,
87, 88, 89, 93, 94, 125(top), 126. 131(bottom). *Brian Blauser*: 91. *Reuters/Wolfgang Rattay/ Archive Photos*:
125(bottom).

Printed in Italy

1   3   5   6   4   2

CONTENTS

WEST VIRGINIA IS . . .

West Virginia is wild . . .

"Here are mountain and ripsnorting river and ripsnorting people who came to conquer them both." —poet Stephen Vincent Benét

"Mountains run up like walls, with little flat land between, and the people who live there like it that way. They have mortal fear, some of them, of country where there are no hills to protect them from the winds." —writer Virgil Carrington Jones

. . . and peaceful.

"The very stillness of the place was beautiful. Poverty, serenity and beauty seemed to go hand in hand through the valley." —longtime Kanawha Valley resident Fanny Zerbe (1928)

West Virginians love to tell stories . . .

"These people were farmers. . . . They brought few books besides the Bible, but in their minds they carried a great store of traditional knowledge and in their hearts a love for the best that had been said in a story and song by their ancestors for countless generations." —folklorist Patrick W. Gainer

. . . and are famous for their friendliness.

"In all my travels over the hills and through the hollows for half a century . . . never have I encountered any sign of hostility, but always a genuine show of friendliness."

—folklorist Patrick W. Gainer

West Virginia is defined by the sharp peaks and narrow valleys of the ancient Appalachian Range. The land is rich in coal, oil, gas, timber, game, and scenic beauty. West Virginia was once a Native American hunting ground. Then came the coal industry, and small communities grew up between mountain ridges. Now the state faces dramatic changes. Towns once isolated by mountainous terrain are connected by information technology. Livelihoods once determined by the need for coal and other minerals are now made by the attractions of a beautiful landscape.

The people of West Virginia are poor and proud, independent and hospitable. The struggle with poverty and isolation has made some leave the state and others feel trapped by it. But many have embraced the state's unique nature and found happiness in its mountains. Often West Virginians are leery of strangers for fear of being misunderstood. But most open their hearts to anyone interested in their beloved state.

1 MOUNTAINOUS WONDERLAND

Over 300 million years ago prehistoric marine life thrived in a sea covering most of what is now West Virginia. The underwater sediment hardened to become a thick rock layer. Then two huge masses of this rock, called tectonic plates, began to shift. Their movement was slow—only a few inches a year—but steady. Over the course of 50 million years it caused some parts of the earth to crack and crumble and others to jut out and up, creating the ridges of the Appalachians.

Rich forests of ancient trees and swamps of peat flourished, and their remains became the vast coal deposits that are still mined in West Virginia. Today, ice and water continue to carve the steep ridges and gouge the deep ravines where rivers even older than the mountains still flow.

THE PANHANDLE STATE

West Virginia is sometimes called the Panhandle State because it is shaped like a large pan with two handles—one in the north and one in the east. Bordered by Ohio on the northwest, Pennsylvania and Maryland on the north, Virginia on the east and south, and Kentucky on the southwest, its boundaries are the most irregular of any state.

The only state lying completely within the Appalachian

LAND AND WATER

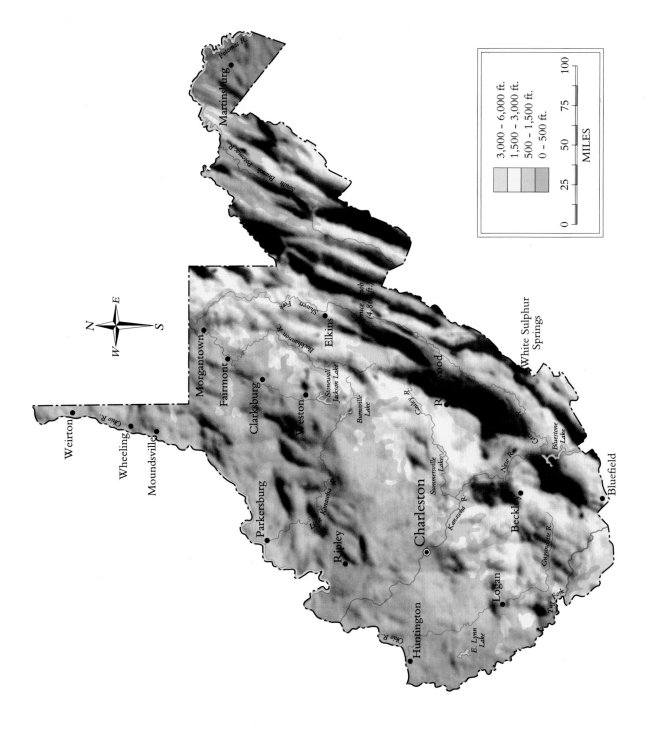

Potomac R.

Martinsburg

South Branch Potomac R.

3,000 - 6,000 ft.
1,500 - 3,000 ft.
500 - 1,500 ft.
0 - 500 ft.

MILES

0   25   50   75   100

Shavers Fork

Spruce Knob
(4,863 ft.)

Elkins

Buckhannon R.

N
W   E
S

Morgantown

Fairmont

Clarksburg

Weston

Stonewall
Jackson Lake

Burnsville
Lake

Greenbrier R.

Ronceverte

White Sulphur
Springs

Bluestone
Lake

Bluefield

Weirton

Ohio R.

Wheeling

Moundsville

Parkersburg

Summersville
Lake

New R.

Beckley

Greenbrier R.

Little Kanawha R.

Ripley

Charleston

Kanawha R.

Logan

Guyandotte R.

Tug Fork

Huntington

Ohio R.

E. Lynn
Lake

Mountain system, West Virginia has three natural regions: the Appalachian Plateau in the west, the ridge and valley region in the east, and the Blue Ridge region at the tip of the eastern panhandle.

The Appalachian Plateau. In the spring, pink, purple, and white rhododendrons (the state flower) bloom where sunlight falls in the dense forests of the Appalachian Plateau. Deep V-shaped river valleys rise and fall across this region, eventually intersecting with the rugged Allegheny Mountains, which divide the plateau from the eastern part of West Virginia. This part of the state challenged early settlers. Altina Waller wrote, "Towering mountains obliterated the sun for many hours a day and impeded travel except along creek beds and rivers." Flat land is rare in this region, but what there is of it is usually populated, even though it is often prone to flooding.

The Appalachian Plateau contains large deposits of coal, oil, gas, salt, and iron ore. The Kanawha Valley breaks up the rural landscape with miles of chemical plants bordering the Kanawha River and surrounding Charleston, the state capital. There, the fresh mountain air is replaced with the smell of industry; valley grasses with cement pavement and asphalt roads.

The Ridge and Valley Region. From the barren, rocky tops of West Virginia's highest peaks you can see how vast and beautiful this country is. The towering mountains roll down to fertile green valleys. This is the ridge and valley region.

Eagles and hawks circle the sky and land on windswept trees. Parts of arctic tundra bogs have found their way there, in places like Dolly Sods and Cranberry Glades. Mountain laurel, which looks like a delicate version of the rhododendron, grows in abundance

Only a few windswept trees survive among the gray boulders at the top of Dolly Sods. During the coldest winter months, it is not unusual for the road through this wilderness to be closed.

just below the rocky peaks, as do huckleberries, which look and taste like blueberries.

This region includes the Allegheny Mountains, which rise along the eastern border with Virginia and most of the eastern panhandle. Ridges are covered with trees and rise to between three and four thousand feet. The valleys have rich soil, which is used for farming. It is awe-inspiring country, full of spectacular vistas and

Hikers must make their way around the spongy bogs found throughout the Allegheny highlands.

lovely meadows. This majestic beauty inspired well-traveled author Pearl Buck to proclaim her native West Virginia the "world's most beautiful place."

The Blue Ridge. "The passage of the Potomac through the Blue Ridge," wrote Thomas Jefferson, "is perhaps one of the most stupendous scenes in nature." Watching the river flow between mountain ridges at the foot of mighty crags, Jefferson wrote that he had the feeling that, long ago, waters had been dammed up in

CRANBERRY GLADES

One of the strangest parts of southwestern West Virginia is Cranberry Glades, a piece of the arctic tundra pushed into Pocahontas County by glaciers millions of years ago. A tundra is a treeless, sometimes boggy plain found in cold, northern climates. Even though the glaciers retreated from West Virginia long ago, when visiting the glades always take along a jacket, because the weather often shifts from warm to cold in an instant.

The Cranberry Glades is a 750-acre bog with a spongy ground made up of partially decayed plants called peat. Visitors must stay on a boardwalk to avoid being ankle-deep in water. To protect the delicate ecosystem, they cannot touch the plants. In the case of the large-leafed skunk cabbage this is an especially good idea, since it smells like its namesake.

Cranberry and insect-eating plants creep along the floor of the bog. The cranberry plants are well camouflaged by their reddish green color. The most unusual part of the glades are the amazing insect-eating plants. These plants do not have teeth. Instead, they trap bugs and then digest them with juices they secrete.

the hills, waters that rose until at last they "broke over at this spot and tore the mountain down from its summit to its base." This narrow V-shaped strip of land is Harpers Ferry, the state's lowest point at 240 feet above sea level.

The Blue Ridge region includes the stunning Shenandoah Valley, full of apple and peach orchards. Even as he was being led to his execution in this area, abolitionist John Brown said to the jailer accompanying him, "This is beautiful country. I never noticed it before."

Harpers Ferry, West Virginia's lowest point, clings to the hillsides along the banks of the Potomac.

FAST-FLOWING RIVERS

When explorers Thomas Batts and Robert Fallam crossed the Appalachian Mountains in 1671 and came upon the New River, they were astonished to find it flowing west. The New is a mysterious, unpredictable, and ancient river, older than the Appalachians. Northeast of the New, rivers flow into the Atlantic Ocean. Southwest of the New, most rivers flow into the Ohio River. When the mountains were thrust up, the New cut its own route, creating spectacular canyons, gorges, and "narrows," which are now highlights of the Appalachian scenery. Some authorities say that at one time even the mighty Mississippi was a tributary of the New. It has changed course and direction since ancient times. Now it flows quietly into the Kanawha, and together these two rivers cut entirely across West Virginia.

The New River is not safe to swim in. Whirlpools can pull unsuspecting swimmers below the water's surface, and the river has a dangerous undertow. But it has become important to the states's growing white-water-rafting industry.

Many people visit West Virginia to ride its rapid rivers. The Gauley River is the ultimate white-water challenge. The ride down the Gauley has been described as "a rollercoaster of rapids with no calm spots in between." In the north, the Cheat, the Tygart, and the south branch of the Potomac are good rivers for rafting and canoeing in the spring. The Shenandoah in the eastern panhandle and the Greenbrier in the south are great for first-time paddlers looking for scenic beauty and historic sights.

"What a rush! I'd like to do that again," exclaimed one white-water rafter *after being retrieved from rapids on the New River.*

NATURE'S AIR-CONDITIONING

West Virginia's variations in altitude cause variations in climate. Thick fog and several feet of snow often cover the mountain peaks. Winter cold and snow hit higher elevations harder. In Elkins, a town with one of the highest elevations in the state, January temperatures range between twenty-two and forty-three degrees. Lower valleys experience little snow, often only twenty inches, which seldom stays on the ground long.

The state capital, Charleston, is located in the Kanawha River valley. During the summer it is considerably warmer and more humid than the surrounding mountains. Many people who work in Charleston live in nearby mountain towns and look forward to going home and escaping the valley's heat and humidity. The air is fresher and more comfortably cool up in the mountains.

Bluefield, a mountain town and West Virginia's southernmost community, calls itself "nature's air-conditioned city." City merchants have vowed to serve free lemonade if the mercury hits ninety degrees. They have gone years without ever having to set up a stand.

West Virginia's mountains provide a cool—and beautiful—retreat from its humid valleys.

FREQUENT FLOODING

Rainfall is plentiful in all parts of the state, and heavy winter and spring floods are not uncommon in the lower valleys. "California has earthquakes, Florida has hurricanes, and West Virginia has flooding," said West Virginia Rivers Coalition executive director Roger Harris. "We have had a major flood event every eighteen months since the state began. It's just part of who we are and where we live."

In 1985, a devastating flood hit the town of Moorefield. "It was like a wall of water coming down" the south fork of the Potomac, said Stanley Trumbo, who lost a barn built in 1870 to the deluge. "The school was covered with mud, the downtown was full of farm implements," said hairdresser Tee Turner. But the crisis brought out the best in this town's resourceful residents. Working together, they found shelter for everyone who had to be evacuated from their homes and started the slow and dirty process of cleaning up the town. "Everyone worked and before long we had our school again and downtown looked normal," said Turner.

PLANT AND ANIMAL LIFE

Hundreds of years ago, West Virginia was covered by magnificent forests. Fires, logging, and pioneer farmers wiped out those once towering woods. Today, second-growth and later-growth trees cover about four-fifths of the state. Evergreen forests of white pine, red spruce, and hemlock cover mountain slopes and border riverbanks.

Cathedral State Park is a majestic stand of virgin hemlock and hardwood trees. These ancient trees are just as they were before man invaded these mountains. A walk through the grove is a little like going back before recorded history. A floor of dark green moss and an abundance of ferns add to the mysterious atmosphere of this park.

Flowers of all kinds can be found in the state. Wildflowers border even newly built highways. Red poppies, purple clover, white daisies, and yellow black-eyed Susans make a drive up Interstate 79 pleasant.

Hundreds of years ago, buffalo, elk, bear, cougar, deer, and other large mammals roamed the state's rugged terrain. After seeing the Kanawha Valley in 1770, George Washington wrote, "This country abounds in Buffalo and wild game of all kinds, as also in all kinds of wild fowl, there being in the bottom a great many small grassy ponds or lakes which are full of swan, geese and ducks."

What Washington saw has changed. Strip-mining and pollution from the chemical industry have killed off much of West Virginia's game and fowl. Most large species have disappeared. However, deer are still very numerous, and black bear have increased their numbers in recent years.

New conservation methods are beginning to bring back some of what Washington found so plentiful. Restored strip-mined and deforested land has insured the survival of many small animals, including beavers, otters, martens, minks, bobcats, foxes, and groundhogs. Similar efforts have brought back fish once endangered by wastes from mines and sawmills. Mountain rivers and streams are again full of trout, walleye, bass, and pike.

West Virginia is alive with songbirds, including cardinals (the state bird), wood thrushes, brown thrashers, and scarlet tanagers.

Black bears may be found in and around West Virginia's state parks.

The bobcat is just one of the many kinds of animals living in West Virginian forests.

Northern copperhead snakes are most often seen in West Virginia's state parks, but sometimes people spot them elsewhere. "We had them in my backyard when I was growing up," said Beckley native Pam Ramsey.

Hawks, eagles, and falcons live on mountain peaks. Quail, woodcocks, and snipes join migratory birds such as loons, ducks, geese, and grebes on small lakes and ponds.

There are lots of snakes in West Virginia—twenty species in all. Two types are poisonous, the timber rattlesnake and the copperhead. Hikers are most likely to see copperheads in the southern West Virginia state parks of Little Beaver, Grandview-Beckley, and Babcock. It is also not unusual to see rattlesnakes in the northern parks of Canaan Valley and Blackwater Falls.

CONSERVATION VERSUS INDUSTRY

Sometimes the need to protect the environment conflicts with the needs of West Virginia's industries. Many large-scale strip mines are located in southern West Virginia. Strip-mining is a method of extracting coal by digging up whole mountaintops rather than tunneling underground. Although strip-mining is a safer, more efficient way to take out coal, it leaves ugly gouges in the earth. The unneeded dirt and rock are deposited in a nearby valley.

Foresters warned decades ago that it would be difficult for trees to grow on strip-mined land. Hardwood forests take eighty to one hundred years to grow. Strip mines turn soil and water systems upside down, making it difficult for forests to regrow. Between 1987 and 1995, nearly 250,000 acres of state timberland were lost to strip-mining, farming, and housing developments. This was the first decrease in state timberland acreage in more than fifty years. "It's just devastating," said State Forestry Division director Bill Maxey, who lamented the "loss in forest growth and wildlife habitat."

Even with all the problems and conservation work that needs to be done, the state is much improved. Laws have been passed to protect the land. For instance, if mining companies destroy a stream, they have to pay to clean it up. The coal companies have become more serious about reviving strip-mined areas.

U.S. Interior Secretary Bruce Babbitt recognized these improvements while visiting the state in 1996. "When I first visited West Virginia in the early 1960s, I saw a lot of landscapes like the one over there," said Babbitt, glancing at a strip-mining operation. "Twenty-five years later, I see a state that has changed. The land-

"There's no other efficient way to get rid of the sludge," said engineer Jim Pierce about strip-mining. "If we want a coal industry in this area, this is a necessary evil."

scape has changed. It is a better landscape in many ways, a different landscape—a savannah of forests coming back, of fields." Babbitt said West Virginia is a "rebuke to those who say, 'It's jobs or the environment.' This landscape shouts out, 'You can have both.'"

2 APPALACHIAN FRONTIER

View on Cheat River, by William Sheridan Young

People first inhabited the Kanawha Valley more than 12,000 years ago. These people, the Paleo-Indians, used sharp stone tools or spearheads called Clovis points to slay large mammals like mammoths, mastodons, and caribou. Archaeologists have found these tools in the mountains and along river bottoms. Paleo-Indians also hunted smaller animals and gathered plants. They moved a lot, following the migration of the herds.

Eventually, the climate grew warmer. Mammoths and mastodons became extinct, and the deer population increased. The people changed too. They did not travel as much, and they used smaller spears for hunting.

NATIVE PEOPLES

Several thousand years ago, the Adena Indians, who are believed to be the ancestors of some modern Native Americans, began building burial mounds. They buried their dead leaders in log tombs and then covered the tombs with a large pile of dirt. Some big mounds have several layers of burials and dirt.

The Adenas were hunters and gatherers. Women and children gathered nuts, roots, berries, seeds, and leaves, while the men went after game. They used nuts and seeds like we use corn and wheat today. Their clothing was probably made of deer hide. Tools were made from stone, bone, wood, even deer antlers. Arrowheads, knives, scrapers, and drills were made from flint—a hard stone found along the banks of the Kanawha River. Pottery was made by digging clay from the riverbank and mixing it with crushed mussel shells.

By about A.D. 1500, the mound builders had abandoned their villages. No one knows exactly what happened, but experts think that warfare, disease, or lack of rain may have forced them to leave their homes.

By the 1640s, the region was primarily a hunting ground for members and allies of the powerful Iroquois Confederacy, a group of eastern Native American tribes that banded together. When the first European settlers arrived in present-day West Virginia in about 1730, a few Tuscaroras, Mingos, Shawnees, and Delawares, who were all connected to the Iroquois Confederacy, lived in the state.

EUROPEAN EXPLORERS

John Lederer, a German physician, is credited with being the first European to see West Virginia. Commissioned by Virginia's governor, Sir William Berkeley, he made two trips to the top of the Blue Ridge in 1669 and 1670. Lederer appears to have been very dramatic and a bit of an exaggerator. His travel journals talk of giant snakes, ravenous wolves, and mountains so high he could see "the Atlantick-Ocean washing the Virginian Shore."

In 1671, Englishmen Thomas Batts and Robert Fallam crossed the mountains and found a river that flowed into the Ohio River. It was probably the New River, or maybe the Tug Fork. This

Young George Washington leads his exhausted troops through western Virginia during the French and Indian War.

discovery helped England claim the Ohio Valley.

Perhaps the most famous early traveler to western Virginia was George Washington. In the late 1740s, at age sixteen, Washington joined a party of surveyors working for Lord Thomas Fairfax, a wealthy Virginia landowner. They crossed the Allegheny Mountains into what is now West Virginia. At that time, Appalachia was the frontier of North America. The people who lived there must have seemed rough and uncultured to young Washington, the son of a wealthy plantation owner. According to Washington, one night, he "went in to ye Bed as they called it when to my Surprise I found it to be nothing [but] a Little Straw matted together without sheets or anything else [but] only one thread[bare] blanket with double its weight of Vermin such as Lice, Fleas." As he got older, Washington grew to love the frontier and respected the hardiness of its settlers.

In 1754, the struggle between the British and the French over territory in North America erupted into open conflict in the French and Indian War. Virginia's colonial governor promised land to men who enlisted to defend the frontier. Washington fought as a commander for the British. After the British won the war, Washington was visited almost daily by men who had served under him and who looked to him to help them claim their land. This was no easy task, because the British government, the Virginia Assembly, and various land companies opposed keeping the promise to the veterans.

Washington left for the Ohio Valley in October 1770, in part to help the former soldiers and in part to attain some land for himself. He succeeded in doing both. Washington planned to return to the frontier in 1773 to begin surveying his land, but he never did.

CONFLICTS WITH SETTLERS

After the French and Indian War, thousands of pioneers made their way to Virginia's western frontier. Many built homes in the Ohio River valley, on land that Indian nations had not given up. As a result, settlers and Native Americans often clashed violently.

One Mingo chief had been particularly friendly with white settlers. He was even baptized a Christian and took the name John Logan. But his sentiments changed. In 1773, a land speculator named Michael Cresap led a group of men on a murderous spree against Shawnees and other Native Americans. On April 30, 1774, some of Cresap's followers massacred a dozen peaceful Mingos. Among those killed was Logan's sister. Logan later maintained that Cresap murdered his entire family, but there is only documented evidence of his sister's death.

Feeling betrayed and vengeful, Logan killed at least thirteen settlers that summer. Later in the fall, he joined forces with a Shawnee chief named Cornstalk to fight the forces of Lord Dunmore, the governor of the Virginia Colony. That conflict, known as Lord Dunmore's War, ended with an Indian defeat at Point Pleasant, on the Ohio River at the western edge of the colony. Cornstalk agreed to a peace treaty with Dunmore's armies. But at its signing he spoke of the Virginians' sins and broken promises and openly accused them of inciting the war.

In 1775, the American Revolution broke out. Most of the Ohio tribes sided with the British, who armed them to fight the rebelling colonists. Still, peace reigned in western Virginia until the spring of 1777—a time often referred to as the Bloody Year of the Three Sevens. Americans were settling land protected by treaties between the British and Native Americans. Because the British did not want rebelling colonists to take over the frontier, they encouraged the Indians to defend their hunting grounds by force.

Cornstalk warned all sides that blood would flow as never before.

CHIEF LOGAN'S LETTER

John Logan did not attend the peace negotiations at Point Pleasant. Instead, he sent a letter expressing his outrage over the actions of the white settlers:

I appeal to any white man to say if ever he entered Logan's cabin hungry and he gave him not meat, if ever he came cold and naked and he clothed him not?

During the course of the last long and bloody war, Logan remained idle in his camp, an advocate for peace. Such was my love for the whites that my countrymen pointed at me as I passed and said "Logan is the friend of the white man." I had even thought to have lived with you but for the injuries of one man. Colonel Cresap, the last spring, in cold blood and unprovoked, murdered all the relations of Logan, not even sparing my women and children. There runs not a drop of my blood in veins of any living creatures. This called on me for revenge. I have killed many. I have fully glutted my vengeance. For my country I rejoice at the beams of the peace; but do not harbor a thought that mine is the joy of fear. Logan never felt fear. He will not turn on his heel to save his life.

Who is there to mourn for Logan? Not one.

He admitted he was powerless to stop it, but still he tried to bring peace. Accompanied by a young Shawnee chief named Red Hawk, the old leader went again to Point Pleasant—this time to warn Captain Matthew Arbuckle about the growing tension between the Shawnee and white settlers. But the two chiefs were taken prisoner and held as hostages. Cornstalk knew that he would likely be killed soon. He said, "When I was young and went to war, I often thought each would be my last adventure and I should return no more. I still live. Now I am in the midst of you and if you choose, you may kill me. I can die but once. It is alike for me whether it is now or hereafter."

Several days later, a white soldier was killed and scalped outside the fort. With a cry of "Let us kill the red dog," a group of soldiers took over the fort. They wanted to kill the captured chiefs and Cornstalk's son, who was visiting him. They threatened Captain Arbuckle with death if he tried to stop them. Cornstalk was warned of the mutiny but made no attempt to escape. Instead, with great dignity he walked toward the murderous men. He took seven bullets in his body before falling to the ground without even a groan. The other two Indians were then slain in cold blood.

INDUSTRY ON THE FRONTIER

After the Revolutionary War, western Virginia was still considered a frontier. This attracted such adventurers as Daniel Boone, who came to the Kanawha Valley in 1788 after losing his holdings in Kentucky. Boone always looked like a frontiersman, carrying a tomahawk and his favorite bear trap, "Old Isaac." Traveling far and

The second siege of Fort Henry in Wheeling is called the last battle of the Revolutionary War. On September 11, 1782, British and Native American troops attacked the American-held fort but were defeated.

near he hunted beavers, otters, foxes, and raccoons.

In 1791, he settled near what would soon become Charleston. He was elected to represent Kanawha County in the state government. The 1790s were a time of peace and transition in western Virginia. Boone resisted the changes. He became restless, longing for new environments to explore and conquer, and in 1795 he left the Kanawha Valley for Missouri.

Industry was developing in the mountains of western Virginia. In 1794, an iron furnace was built at King's Creek. The first salt well was drilled in the Kanawha Valley in 1806. By 1808, salt production had increased from 150 to 1,250 pounds a day. At

The saltworks on the Kanawha River was the first step in developing the chemical industry in West Virginia.

about the same time, oil and natural gas were discovered in the region, and the first steamboat began operating on the Ohio River, opening up water transportation in the area.

As western Virginia grew in population, it developed much differently than the rest of Virginia. There weren't any large plantations or wealthy landowners in western Virginia. The area's economy was based on industry, not agriculture.

The people in the western region became increasingly unhappy with their parent state. For the most part, people in the west were not slaveholders. Many openly opposed slavery. They also felt their needs were ignored by Virginia's government. As early as 1810, western Virginians had officially protested that they were not getting equal representation in the Virginia legislature.

Then in 1859 something happened in the town of Harpers Ferry. There, the Potomac and Shenandoah Rivers meet, and Virginians with strong views on slavery split. And there, a spark helped ignite a war, dividing a state and a nation.

JOHN BROWN'S RAID

Abolitionist minister Henry Ward Beecher called him a "crazed old man." African-American leader Frederick Douglass found him eloquent. Confederate general Thomas "Stonewall" Jackson thought him a brave but misguided man. And French writer Victor Hugo said "he was an apostle and a hero. [His death] has only increased his glory, and made him a martyr."

John Brown referred to himself as a "determined abolitionist" who swore "eternal war with slavery." His description rings true. Even before Harpers Ferry, he led raids into Kansas in which proslavery advocates were captured and killed.

Brown came to Harpers Ferry hoping to start a slave rebellion in Virginia. On Sunday, October 16, 1859, Brown, five black men, and sixteen white men prepared to raid the federal arsenal in town. At midnight, they headed toward the arsenal, cutting telegraph wires and taking sixty hostages on their way. Brown expected to exchange hostages for local slaves willing to fight for the cause. But hostage Patrick Higgins escaped and alerted the town. Ironically, the first fatality was a free black man, Heyward Shepherd, who wandered into the area and was shot trying to flee.

John Brown started out as a peaceful abolitionist. It wasn't until 1839 that he pledged "an active war on slavery."

Marines storm the engine house to capture Brown and his men.

Late Monday morning, eighty marines led by Robert E. Lee attacked the arsenal. Brown and his men retreated to the engine house, a small brick building on the arsenal grounds. Within a day, the marines captured the engine house, and John Brown's raid at Harpers Ferry was over. Seventeen men had died in the battle, including Brown's sons, Oliver and Watson. Only five slaves were freed as a result of the incident. They had been owned by the mayor of Harpers Ferry, who was slain in the raid. His will insured their freedom.

John Brown was tried and found guilty of treason, first-degree murder, and conspiring and advising with slaves and others to rebel. On December 2, 1859, he was hanged. Six other raiders were also tried for treason and executed.

John Brown's raid did not accomplish what Brown had hoped it would, but it did further the abolitionists' cause by making more people aware of it. It also angered people who were for slavery and helped push the nation towards war. On the day of his death, Brown wrote, "I, John Brown am now quite certain that the crimes of this guilty land: will never be purged away: but with Blood. I had as I now think: vainly flattered myself that without very much bloodshed, it might be done."

Brown was right. A sea of blood would be spilled before slavery came to an end. In fact, more Americans died in the Civil War than in all other wars this country has fought combined.

THE CIVIL WAR AND A NEW STATE

In 1861, eleven Southern states seceded (removed themselves)

LIVING THROUGH THE CIVIL WAR

Many West Virginians found themselves caught in the middle of the Civil War, facing divided families and loyalties. The diary of French Creek teenager Sirene Bunton illustrates the tensions of the era. Though living in what was still part of Virginia (a state that seceded), most people Sirene knew were sympathetic to the Union cause. But there were always exceptions, and Sirene's brother-in-law Fenton Payne was one. "To think one of our family is a traitor to our country," Sirene lamented in June 1863.

Payne was a Confederate sympathizer who paid for his beliefs with his life. Despite her Union loyalties, Sirene was sorry about Payne's death: "July 3, 1863. Some dreadful news if true. Fenton Payne and Skid Ferril were killed by our men. They were going to Dixie but they have gone to their account. I sincerely pity Sister Elsey. I wish I could go and see her. She is left with seven small children and what is to become of them I don't know. . . . It is awful times."

Sirene knew the fear of losing friends and loved ones to the fight. Her three brothers fought with Union forces, and the eldest, Birney, died in the war. Sometimes that fear overwhelmed the fifteen-year-old: "July 6, 1863. All the troops left town last night at nine o'clock for Webster. I expect the citizens of Buchanan are badly frightened now. The [Confederates] surrounded our [troops] at Beverly, took them prisoners and then killed them in cold blood. . . . The rebels are perfect savages to kill men in that way. I hope they will get their pay for it before they get out of West Virginia."

from the Union and formed the Confederate States of America. It was the beginning of the Civil War.

When western Virginians learned that the state of Virginia had voted to secede, they held mass protest meetings and proceeded to create their own state. Delegates from the western counties met at Wheeling on June 11, 1861. There they formed the Restored Government of Virginia with Francis H. Pierpont as governor. Pierpont's first act was to ask President Abraham Lincoln for military support. When that was granted, it made the Restored Government at Wheeling the legal government of Virginia. In October 1861, people of the western counties voted overwhelmingly to form a new state. Two years later, West Virginia became the nation's thirty-fifth state.

West Virginia was the site of many Civil War battles. The eastern panhandle bore much of the fighting. The town of Romney changed

Francis H. Pierpont became governor of the Restored Government of Virginia in 1861.

)

hands fifty-six times. Conflicting loyalties split families and friendships. It has been estimated that West Virginia contributed 28,000 to 36,000 soldiers to the Union army and 9,000 to 12,000 to the Confederate army.

A STATE OF INDUSTRY

After the war, a spiral of prosperity began in West Virginia. Railroads stimulated industries, which in turn increased the need for coal. Soon, coal became king.

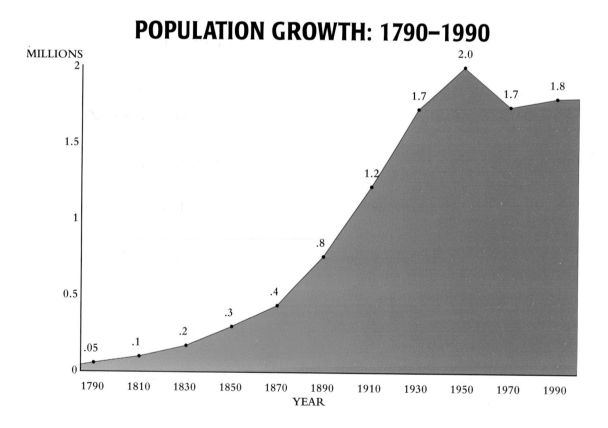

POPULATION GROWTH: 1790–1990

The mining life was difficult. Booker T. Washington, a former slave who would later found the Tuskegee Institute, moved to West Virginia right after the war. He worked many jobs in Malden, West Virginia, but found coal mining the most grueling. He wrote, "it was a very hard job to get one's skin clean after the day's work was over. . . . I do not believe that one ever experiences anywhere else such darkness as he does in a coal-mine. . . . I many times found myself lost in the mine. To add to the horror of being lost, sometimes my light would go out and then, if I did not happen to have a match, I would wander about in the darkness until by chance I found some one to give me a light."

Mining was not only hard and dirty but also dangerous. Coal dust that collects in the mines causes a deadly disease called black lung. And sometimes poisonous gases would build up, causing explosions that killed hundreds of miners. In the early 1900s, more coal miners died on the job in West Virginia than in any other state in the country.

Mary Behner worked helping miners and their families at Scott's Run, a group of coal camps near Morgantown in the northern part of the state. In her diary, she described how cheap life was in the 1930s coal camps. After one explosion, she wrote, "There was little we could do at The Shack but pacify the crowds that came along to learn of the progress the rescue crews were making. There was a tension among the miners because all knew that it could have easily been the man in their family. Crowds remained at the mouth of the mine for hours in hopes the bodies would be recovered alive. Many of the wives of the rescue crew waited for fear something might happen to them while working, for there was news that

THE LEGEND OF JOHN HENRY

They say the night he was born lightning struck and the earth trembled. He was black as coal, weighed forty-four pounds, and had a booming voice like a preacher.

John Henry grew to be a big workingman with two ringing hammers and a rainbow round him. He came to West Virginia to drive a hole in a mountain—a hole so big a railroad could go through. Then a boss man came with a new machine called a steam drill. "It can hammer faster and harder than ten men and it never has to stop and rest," he said.

John Henry said, "Let's have a contest. Your steam drill against me and my hammers."

"Okay!" said the boss. "You start on the other side of the mountain and I'll start here. Whoever gets to the middle first wins."

When John Henry swung his hammers through the air, they shone like silver, and when they hit rock, they rang like gold.

All through the night John Henry and the steam drill went at it. As the sun came up, John Henry broke through and met the steam drill. He had come a mile and a quarter; the steam drill only a quarter. Folks cheered, "John Henry! John Henry!"

John Henry walked out of the tunnel, raised his arms over his head, a hammer in each hand. He closed his eyes and fell to the ground.

John Henry was dead. He had hammered so hard and so fast and so long that his big heart had burst.

The next morning they put John Henry on a flatbed railroad car, and the train made its way slowly out of the mountains. All along the way folks lined the tracks, cheering through their tears, "John Henry! John Henry!"

John Henry is dead and buried. But sometimes at night in the mountains you can hear someone singing and hammers ringing.

another explosion might occur any moment."

Although there was money to be made in coal mining, it was not the miner who reaped the rewards. The only time Mary Behner saw coal miners and their families wearing reasonably new clothes was at funerals—often the funerals of mine accident victims.

Many West Virginia coal miners thought that by banding together they could change their poor working conditions. They joined a workers' organization, or union, called the United Mine Workers of America (UMWA). To get what they wanted they agreed among themselves to stop working, or go out on strike.

Mining companies were angered by the strikes. They forced new employees to sign papers agreeing not to join the union and hired guards to prevent union organizers from talking with miners. Miners who did join the UMWA were sometimes beaten up by company guards or locked out of their homes, which were usually owned by the coal mining companies. Still, by 1920, 45,000 West Virginia miners belonged to the UMWA.

Coal was not the only industry growing in West Virginia. During World War I, Germany and the United States were on opposite sides of the conflict, so chemicals could not be imported from Germany, as they traditionally had been. Instead, the Kanawha Valley, with its plentiful resources like salt, became the site of many chemical plants. The federal government constructed a high explosives plant at Nitro and a mustard gas plant at Belle. Nitro, a town of about 25,000 people and 3,400 buildings, sprang up almost overnight in 1918.

Fanny Zerbe, who saw it all happen, wrote, "Gone were the green

JOHN HARDY

A hundred years ago, West Virginia could be a rough and violent place. This song is based on the true story of John Hardy, who was executed for murder on January 19, 1894.

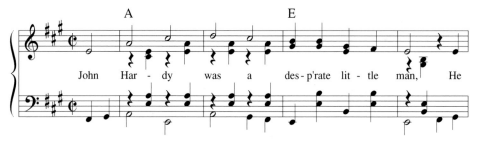

John Har - dy was a des - p'rate lit - tle man, He

wore two guns ev - 'ry day. He shot down a

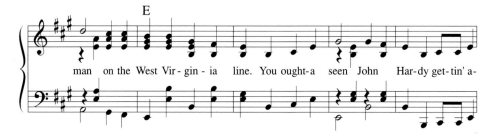

man on the West Vir - gin - ia line. You ought-a seen John Har-dy get-tin' a-

way, poor boy, You ought-a seen John Har - dy get-tin' a-way.

John Hardy stood at the gambling table.
Didn't have no interest in the game.
Up stepped a yellow gal and threw a dollar down,
Said, "John Hardy's playing in my name."

John Hardy took that yellow gal's money,
And then he began to play.
Said, "The man that wins my yellow gal's dollar,
I'll lay him in his lonesome grave."

John Hardy drew to a four-card straight,
And the cowboy drew to a pair.
John failed to catch and the cowboy won,
And he left him sitting dead in his chair.

John started to catch that east-bound train,
So dark he could not see.
Up stepped the police and took him by the arm,
Said, "Johnny, come and go with me."

John Hardy's father came to see him,
Come for to go his bail.
No bail was allowed for a murdering man,
So they shoved John Hardy back in jail.

They took John Hardy to the hanging ground,
And hung him there to die,
And the very last words I heard him say
Were, "My forty-four never told a lie."

"I've been to the east and I've been to the west,
I've travelled this whole world around.
I've been to the river and I've been baptized,
And now I'm on my hanging ground."

Coal mining is dirty, dangerous work. Many miners joined the United Mine Workers of America, which tried to protect workers' rights.

fields, the quiet days, and the beauty and serenity of life. In their place there had appeared overnight the dirt, the noise, and the ugliness of life. The fields became streets of cement pavements and asphalt roads over which thousands of cars and thousands of pairs of feet passed daily. A miracle had happened. Overnight the few farms had been made into a city. . . . An impossibility had occurred."

The prosperity that came with these industries was short-lived. In 1929, the Great Depression hit. Across the country, banks failed, businesses closed, and millions of workers lost their jobs.

The Mountain State suffered even more than the rest of the country. The percentage of people without jobs was higher in West Virginia than in most other states. The state's UMWA membership dwindled to one thousand. More than 80,000 West Virginia miners were unemployed.

To help West Virginians, the U.S. government created new jobs. Workers were hired to build and clear hiking paths through the state's forests. Some people were able to become farmers through one government program aimed at helping the beleaguered people living in the Scott's Run coal camps.

This project meant a new life for many. People traded huts on slag

Clothes were distributed to needy families at the Scott's Run coal camps. When First Lady Eleanor Roosevelt visited the camps in 1933, she found conditions so distressing that "democracy itself was at stake."

heaps—mounds of mining waste—for white cottages with gardens. They grew their own food, so their diet was healthier. And farming offered them a chance to earn a living on their own, escaping the boom-and-bust life of a coal camp.

Journalist William E. Brooks wrote that this new community offered people the chance to "face to the sky instead of to the earth, to watch the long summer wane, and the color come on the moun-

In 1972, a flood of mine waste ripped through Buffalo Creek, destroying most of the surrounding valley. After the disaster, new regulations were put into effect in hopes that the tragedy would never be repeated.

tains, and the snow fall and pass, and the redbud turn the hills to new splendor and the dogwood fleck them with white, instead of being shut away among the slag pile down in one of the 'hallows.'"

FROM KING COAL TO NOW

Coal continues to be an important industry in West Virginia. While changes have made coal mining safer, it is still the most dangerous industrial job. In 1972, in the last major mining disaster in the state, a dam holding back mine waste gave way, creating a thirty-foot-high wave of 30 million gallons of water. It rushed through the valley of Buffalo Creek in Logan County, wiping out sixteen small communities and killing at least 125 people.

Today, West Virginians are facing new challenges: how to bring in different industries that provide more jobs, how to make the state more attractive to travelers, and how to improve education and health services for a rural population. The future looks bright as these challenges are being met one by one.

3 WORKING TOGETHER

The capitol in Charleston

Forty years ago, Cecil H. Underwood became West Virginia's youngest governor. He served the state for two terms. In 1996, at age seventy-four, Underwood was elected again. This time he became the state's oldest governor.

In his inaugural address, he remarked on how different times are now, yet how many of the state's problems remain the same. According to Underwood, too much of the state's politics has been built on conflict and division—labor vs. management, urban vs. rural, north vs. south, and east vs. west. Conflict has made for a lively political scene, but consensus has been best for solving the most difficult problems.

INSIDE GOVERNMENT

Like the federal system, West Virginia has three branches of government: executive, legislative, and judicial.

Executive. The governor is the state's chief executive. He or she appoints many officials and proposes the state budget, which the state legislature then must agree to. A governor may veto (reject) laws or parts of laws passed by the state legislature. But the legislature can override a veto by a majority vote in both houses.

Other elected executive officials are the secretary of state, auditor, treasurer, attorney general, and commissioner of agriculture. Like the

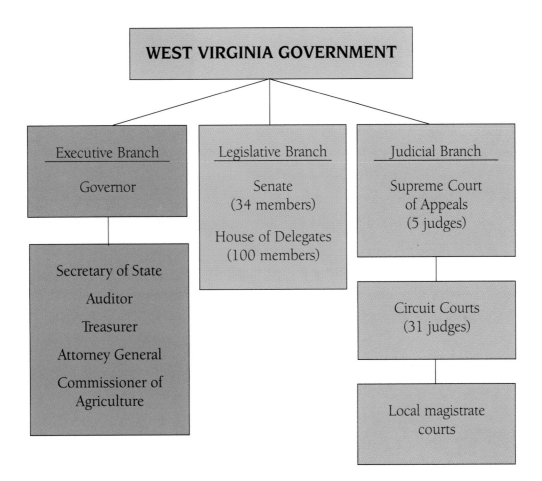

WEST VIRGINIA GOVERNMENT

Executive Branch

Governor

Secretary of State

Auditor

Treasurer

Attorney General

Commissioner of Agriculture

Legislative Branch

Senate
(34 members)

House of Delegates
(100 members)

Judicial Branch

Supreme Court
of Appeals
(5 judges)

Circuit Courts
(31 judges)

Local magistrate
courts

governor, all are elected for four-year terms. There is no lieutenant governor in West Virginia. If a governor dies or is too sick to govern, the office is filled by the president of the state senate until a new governor can be elected.

Sometimes a governor's leadership can have a great impact on the state. For instance, W. Gaston Caperton III, who was first elected in 1989, helped bring about much of West Virginia's recent economic progress. During Caperton's administration, many jobs were created. Factories like the Kanawha Valley's Toyota engine plant came to the state. Road construction during his administration made the state more accessible to visitors and natives alike.

Legislative. The legislature makes new laws and changes old ones. Legislators argue about proposed laws, called bills. When both the state senate and the house of delegates agree to a bill, it is sent to the governor. If the governor signs the bill, it becomes law. The thirty-four state senators are elected for four-year terms. The one hundred members of the house of delegates are elected for two-year terms.

Judicial. West Virginia's court system has three levels. The highest is the Supreme Court of Appeals. It has five justices, who are elected for twelve-year terms. Most of the cases heard by the supreme court are appeals from lower courts. The supreme court also rules on whether the actions of the executive and legislative branches are constitutional.

The state's major trial courts are called circuit courts. Circuit judges are elected to eight-year terms. The number of judges in each circuit varies from one to seven depending on the size of the population it serves. Crimes that can be punished by long prison sentences must be tried in circuit courts. At the lowest level are magistrate and municipal courts. Magistrates can decide civil suits involving up to three thousand dollars. Municipal courts deal with minor offenses such as traffic violations. The state also has family law masters, appointed by the governor, who deal with family matters such as divorce, child adoption, and child-support payments.

OLD AND NEW INDUSTRY

For a long time, West Virginians struggled with high unemploy-

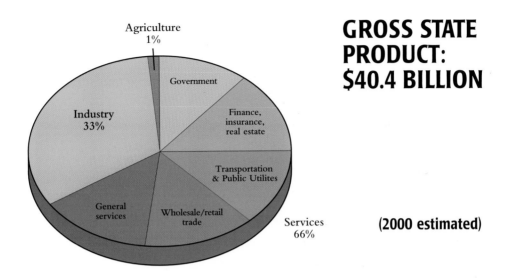

GROSS STATE PRODUCT: $40.4 BILLION

Agriculture 1%

Government

Finance, insurance, real estate

Industry 33%

Transportation & Public Utilites

General services

Wholesale/retail trade

Services 66%

(2000 estimated)

ment and poverty. But in recent years, the tide has begun to turn and the economy is getting better.

Mining and manufacturing were once the mainstay of West Virginia's economy. While they are still important, tourism has become the state's leading industry. In the past, traditional industries harmed the state by polluting its air and water, wreaking havoc on its forests, and leaving ugly gouges in once beautiful mountains. Tourism, however, thrives when the state's natural splendor is preserved.

Manufacturing is the state's second-largest industry. Chemicals are the state's top product. Soap, paint, dye, rubber, and plastic are all made in West Virginia.

Glassmaking has a long history in West Virginia. The state has been home to more than five hundred glass factories. Blenko Glass Company in Milton is famous for producing fine stained glass. Blenko glassmakers must train for years to produce this material

Maintaining a beautiful and clean environment is crucial to West Virginia's thriving tourist industry.

correctly. Blenko Glass can be found in many of the nation's best-known churches, such as the Washington National Cathedral in Washington, D.C., and the Cathedral of St. John the Divine in New York City.

Mining employs only about 31,000 West Virginians now. Still, only four states have more miners. Natural gas, oil, and salt are mined in West Virginia. Although the state still ranks third in the country in mining coal, only about 4 percent of the state's popu-

Glassmaking is an art in West Virginia.

lation is involved in the coal industry, because new technologies require less labor.

Despite its rural landscape, West Virginia is not a big state for agriculture, because there is little flat land to grow produce. But in the eastern panhandle apples and peaches are popular crops. The state ranks ninth in the country in growing apples and tenth in growing peaches. West Virginia farmers were the first to produce Golden Delicious apples.

Many women have joined the ranks of West Virginia's coal miners.

LEAVING DEHUE

Coal mining built Dehue hollow. Now it has destroyed it.

"This used to be the prettiest camp around," says Lena Adkins on the last night she will sleep in the house she has called home for forty-two years.

"My son lives up in Delaware, and he says, 'Mom, I just love to come home and sit in the old porch swing.' He was here two weeks ago, and he just couldn't get over the fact that it's the last time he'll see this place."

Strip mines on either side of the hollow are forcing residents out. The waste from the mining operations is burying the town. The company that owns Dehue's houses and land has offered residents a buyout plan.

In the 1920s, the Youngstown Mining Corporation had built the houses for its workers, who in turn paid rent to the company. Delores Riggs Davis of Kirtland, Ohio, described the town's heyday as a magical time, when people from many different cultures came together. "Some came directly from Ellis Island to find work in Dehue," said Davis.

Forty-seven-year-old Tennis Vernatter took a break from moving to reflect on the town's demise. "It's a part of West Virginia history that's leaving," he said. "But I guess that's called progress."

EDUCATION AND COMMUNITIES

Schools and education are important to West Virginians. Governor Cecil H. Underwood refers to reforming the state's education system as "an annual passion." The problem is not recognizing the need to make the state's public education system better; it is agreeing on how to do it.

Consolidating several schools under one roof and abandoning the smaller school buildings is one way to make each school better equipped. Consolidated schools can offer students more. For instance, they might be able to offer advanced science classes or three foreign languages instead of just one. While consolidation makes a lot of sense in urban areas, it sometimes has unfortunate consequences in rural ones.

For many rural communities separated by steep ridges and deep valleys, schools are the place to gather. They are used by everyone in

Technology is important to education in West Virginia because, says Governor Cecil H. Underwood, computers and the Internet "can reach students in the most isolated areas of the state."

town, not just the students. In many cases, they provide a place to hold meetings and festivals, to stage theater, and play basketball. Schools are also a big source of pride. Rural residents come to the school to cheer on local sports teams and meet with neighbors. If the schools are shut down, the communities lose their center and focus.

The issue has caused fierce debate in most of the state's rural communities. "You always hear a lot about this issue," said Pam Ramsey, a newspaper editor in Beckley. Despite the dissent from rural residents, many county school systems have decided that consolidation is worth it. Still, many people feel their communities have lost a lot while the students have gained.

A CHANCE TO STAY

West Virginia has been called one of the nation's most popular places to be from. The state was one of only seven to lose population between 1980 and 1990.

Most former Mountaineers, as West Virginians are known, left the state to seek jobs elsewhere. There have been two major migrations from the state. In the 1950s, mechanization threw thousands of coal miners out of work. Most went to northern industrial cities like Detroit, Akron, and Cleveland. Then, in the mid-1980s, the lagging coal industry and a nationwide recession sent many West Virginians south looking for jobs in places like Charlotte, North Carolina.

The recent growth of the state's tourist industry has proved how attractive a place West Virginia can be. But if people are to stay in

EARNING A LIVING

Agriculture

- Beef Cattle
- Dairy Products
- Fruit
- Poultry

Industry

- Chemicals & Plastic
- Pottery
- Steel

Natural Resources

- Coal
- Natural Gas
- Oil

Weirton
Wheeling
Moundsville
Morgantown
Fairmont
Martinsburg
Parkersburg
Clarksburg
Weston
Elkins
Ripley
Stonewall
Jackson Lake
Burnsville
Lake
Huntington
Charleston
Summersville
Lake
Richwood
E. Lynn
Lake
Logan
Beckley
White Sulphur
Springs
Bluestone
Lake
Bluefield

Ohio R.
Little Kanawha R.
Buckhannon R.
Shavers Fork
South Branch Potomac R.
Potomac R.
Ohio R.
Gauley R.
Kanawha R.
New R.
Greenbrier R.
Guyandotte R.
Tug Fork

the state, they must have jobs. The state government and business organizations are working hard to bring in new industry by promoting the state as a good place to do business. Improving the education and technological skills of today's students will provide better workers for new industry. The new slogan for the West Virginia Manufacturers' Association is "A Chance to Stay."

Although most people who now live in West Virginia were born in West Virginia, a few outsiders have chosen to move there. Some people have come to the state to live, but work elsewhere. Jefferson County, in the tip of the eastern panhandle, is home to many commuters who work in the Washington, D.C., area.

Others have found livelihoods as well as homes in West Virginia. Craftsman Brian Van Nostrand is from New Jersey. Several years ago he and his family moved to a mountaintop near Hacker Valley, where he built his own studio and pottery kiln. Van Nostrand has found ample seams of clay to dig and use for his creations. West Virginia is a place where he can do the kind of work he wants and live in the kind of surroundings he loves.

Many other people share his enthusiasm. Singer-songwriter Larry Groce says, "We arrived in West Virginia in October of 1972 for a nine month stay that has lasted twenty-four years so far."

4 PROUD MOUNTAINEERS

West Virginians are different from people in other states because West Virginia is different. Sometimes West Virginians feel misunderstood by outsiders. And in the past, few outsiders took the time to get to know these Mountaineers. In 1969, Muriel Miller Dressler wrote:

"I am Appalachia! In my veins
Runs Fierce Mountain pride: the hill-fed streams
Of passion: and, stranger, you don't know me!"

SMALL TOWNS

Unlike most states in the United States, the majority of the 1,840,000 people in West Virginia live in rural areas. (Only Vermont is less urban.) Many hollows, as the state's smallest communities are called, began as small coal mining camps. Unlike most American industries, mining thrives outside of cities.

Even West Virginia's cities do not resemble cities in other states, because they do not have large populations. No metropolitan area in the state has more than 60,000 people, and most people know their neighbors.

Most city dwellers are happy for the work and opportunities their towns provide. But, like their rural cousins, they have favorite ridges and overlooks to escape to that are just a short drive away. It is the beauty of Appalachia that brought people to West Virginia. It is that same beauty that keeps people here and brings others back time and again.

KEEPING THEIR HERITAGE ALIVE

Early immigrants to West Virginia were poor, hard-working people. They came for the natural resources. Farmers found rich soil in the

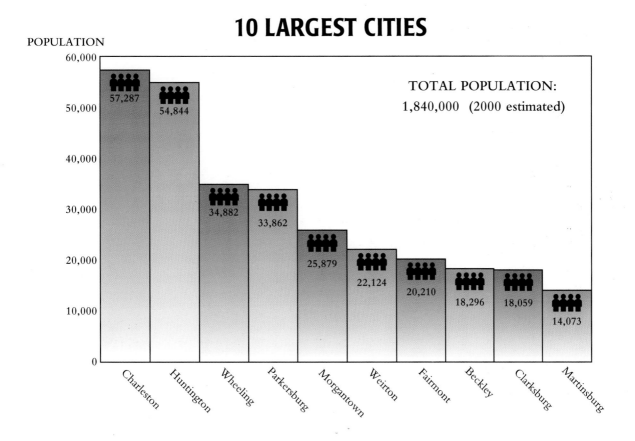

10 LARGEST CITIES

POPULATION

TOTAL POPULATION:
1,840,000 (2000 estimated)

City	Population
Charleston	57,287
Huntington	54,844
Wheeling	34,882
Parkersburg	33,862
Morgantown	25,879
Weirton	22,124
Fairmont	20,210
Beckley	18,296
Clarksburg	18,059
Martinsburg	14,073

Tucked away in the Appalachian hills are small communities called hollows.

valleys. Hunters found plenty of deer and smaller game. All found a place where independence and freedom were honored.

These early settlers were proud that the rugged terrain didn't get the better of them. Pride also came from their love for their new home, the peace they found on the mountaintops, and the livelihoods they earned from hard work in the valleys.

Most early settlers came from Germany or the British Isles. The Appalachian hills often reminded them of where they were born. Today, travelers sometimes have similar reactions. One Scottish visitor to the Mountain State Arts and Crafts Fair in Ripley smiled as he looked at the surrounding peaks. "With the mist on these mountains, it feels like I'm home," he said.

After the Civil War, thousands of Italian, Russian, Polish, and Hungarian immigrants came to West Virginia to work in the coal, logging, and railroad industries. Many African Americans seeking jobs also arrived from Southern states.

Since the early twentieth century, few immigrants from foreign countries have settled in West Virginia. Consequently, almost all Mountaineers today were born in the United States. About 3 percent of West Virginians are African Americans. Less than 1 percent are Hispanic. Only about 1,600 Native Americans and small numbers of Asians live in West Virginia.

Many ethnic groups celebrate their heritage with festivals. Every year in late August or early September, the West Virginia Italian Heritage Festival is held in Clarksburg. Singers, dancers, and puppeteers dressed in colorful costumes provide entertainment. There is also plenty of great Italian food, such as calzones—folded and filled pizzas—for hungry visitors to enjoy.

ETHNIC WEST VIRGINIA

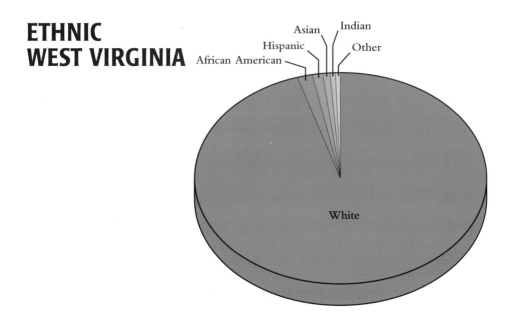

Asian   Indian

Hispanic   Other

African American

White

Many West Virginians can trace their ancestry to the frontier days of the state. Then villages were places for extended families, or clans, to gather. Annual clan reunions are still popular in the state. Some get-togethers attract thousands of loosely related people. The Lilly family reunion is a major event in Flat Top every year. "The Lillys are extremely proud of their heritage, what they've accomplished and who they were," said Daniel Lilly, who is a sixth-generation descendant of the first Lilly pioneers who settled in Flat Top in 1732. After living in Rhode Island for twenty-one years, Lilly decided to move back home. "We all want to go back to our roots," he said. "Heritage is important because the future of our world is based on our past." In recent years the reunion's attendance has dwindled. In its heyday in the 1930s, as many as 75,000 people came to the Flat Top get-together.

CHASING AWAY WINTER

Tucked away in West Virginia's Allegheny Mountains, a bit of Switzerland thrives.

Goat bleats and a babbling creek are the loudest sounds in Helvetia. But as longtime resident and proprietor of the Beekeeper Inn Eleanor Mailloux likes to say: "There are occasional bursts of activity here."

Fasnacht is an old Swiss ritual Helvetians observe every year. It is celebrated one Saturday each February with a Swiss feast and foot-tapping Appalachian music. The townspeople and visitors don costumes for a masked ball. The scarier the costumes the better, because the idea is to drive away the snow, ice, and chill winds.

At the end of the day, a life-size figure stuffed with hay and firecrackers representing Old Man Winter is brought out. It is burned at a bonfire to make way for spring.

Just like the seasons, Fasnacht comes around every year, but Helvetia always remains the same. Its residents like it that way. "We're all in favor of progress, if you don't make any changes," said Mailloux.

The Italian Heritage Festival in Clarksburg is one of the state's best-attended ethnic celebrations.

Often members of the same family stay in one West Virginia town for generations. There is a story about a West Virginia doctor, who was visiting out-of-state and met a woman whose sister-in-law lived in the Appalachian community of Union. "I bet her name is Wikel," said the doctor. The surprised woman said it was and asked the doctor how he knew. "Well, from Union, it had to be either Wikel, or Parker, or Pence," he replied.

APPALACHIAN CULTURE

The Augusta Heritage Center at Davis and Elkins College in Randolph County is keeping the art and music produced by Appalachia's early settlers alive. Both bluegrass and country music have origins in Appalachian culture. Appalachian arts and crafts are made from natural resources like wood, glass, and clay. Most works are made to be used—furniture, quilts, jars, and clay pots.

The center connects Appalachian craftspeople, artists, musicians, and dancers with people eager to carry on these rich traditions. Students can learn wood carving, basket making, glassblowing, quilting, or even clogging, a kind of tap dancing with heavy wooden shoes. Musicians study how to play the fiddle or dulcimer, a sweet-sounding stringed instrument which looks a little like a cross between a harp and a guitar. The center provides a common ground for people of many backgrounds to meet.

THE HILLBILLY IMAGE

Most West Virginians bristle at the prejudiced view some outsiders have of them. Too often they are characterized as uneducated and unsophisticated. They are called hillbillies. To many, just the word hillbilly brings up an image of a barefoot, rifle-toting illiterate— the Hatfield half of the Hatfield-McCoy feud.

No one knows exactly why the infamous battle between a Kentucky family, the McCoys, and a West Virginia family, the Hatfields, started. But it captured the attention of the nation and helped perpetuate the hillbilly image of mountain folk. Ignored is

Traditional crafts like basket weaving are a vital part of the Augusta experience.

the fact that the Hatfields ended up a wealthy and respected family. Henry Drury Hatfield became governor of the state. Matewan police chief Sid Hatfield became a folk hero who defended the rights of impoverished and exploited coal miners in the early twentieth century.

Many West Virginian potters dig their own clay from seams in nearby mountains.

FRIED RAMPS

Spring in Appalachia brings sweet-smelling flowers and just plain smelly ramps.

Ramps are wild leeks, which are related to onions. They grow in West Virginia's mountains between April and June. Families get together and fry up some ramps along a stream or at home. All over the state there are ramp festivals, the most famous being Richwood's Feast of the Ramson.

The late Jim Comstock, longtime editor of *West Virginia Hillbilly* magazine, once said about his favorite delicacy: "One of the nice things about ramps—maybe the only nice thing—is that one who eats them can't smell another who had, and that one thing makes a town better to live in when everybody (almost) turns out and eats the stinkers."

Ask an adult to help you make fried ramps. If you don't happen to live in West Virginia, you can substitute leeks or green onions.

1. Wash ramps really well and cut off roots.

2. Cut ramps into thirds.

3. Cook bacon in a large skillet and put aside.

4. Add the cut ramps to the bacon grease and cook until tender.

5. Crumble the bacon and add to the ramps.

Serve with brown beans, corn bread, and brown pop (like cola or root beer).

West Virginia writer Don West believes too many people think hillbillies are shallow-minded racists. "They don't remember that tens of thousands of southern Appalachian men volunteered for the Union in the Civil War," said West. "How many people know that one reason why West Virginia became a state was that the hillbillies rejected the idea of slavery?"

At least one West Virginian has embraced the title of hillbilly. In the 1950s, Jim Comstock founded the *West Virginia Hillbilly*, "a newspaper for people who can't read, edited by an editor who can't edit." Comstock maintained that what West Virginia needed was, "a cheap, unsophisticated country weekly to buck it up, and say some kind words about it now and then, and wrap up its history and colorful lore, and spank it when it gets ugly." The feisty editor took on issues like bigotry, corruption, discrimination, and greed with help from Ma, Pa, and Fiddlin' Clyde, a fictional hillbilly family whose ignorance serves to enlighten readers. Despite the Richwood publication's down-home humor, it was declared "sophisticated" by *Saturday Review* magazine. Comstock demanded a retraction.

Comstock's other accomplishments include preserving a steam railroad, building a hospital, saving the home of author Pearl Buck, creating an annual Past 80 Party for "People With No Quittin' Sense At All," and encouraging everyone to eat ramps. Although Comstock has died, the *West Virginia Hillbilly* lives on. But it will never be quite the same.

5 MAKING THEIR MARK

Mountaineers have gained fame for accomplishments in many different fields, from business and aviation to arts and sports.

MOUNTAINEER TYCOON

Donald F. Duncan was a self-made man who will forever be associated with the yo-yo. He was born in 1891 and grew up in Huntington, at the western edge of West Virginia. Duncan had to leave school in the eighth grade to help support his family after his father died. From such humble beginnings, he managed to make a small fortune by the time he was thirty.

Duncan was a born salesman and a promotional genius. He invented the Eskimo Pie, originated the Good Humor ice cream truck, and developed "premium incentives"—"Kids, just send in two boxtops and receive free one . . ."

In the late 1920s, he bought the Flores Yo-Yo Company along with the "yo-yo" trademark, for a reported $25,000. Duncan yo-yos were born.

To sell the toy, he talked his way past the servants at the home of newspaper tycoon William Randolph Hearst, who owned a chain of papers scattered across the country. "I have a great plan to stimulate circulation," Duncan told Hearst, "I can get new readers for your papers." Duncan suggested setting up demonstrations and yo-yo contests in towns with Hearst newspapers. Prizes like bicycles and baseball gloves would be given away to the winners. But in order to be eligible, kids would have to bring in three six-month subscriptions to Hearst-owned newspapers. Both the yo-yos and subscriptions sold like hotcakes.

MAKING A DIFFERENCE

Just one year before the end of the Civil War, the founder of Mother's Day was born. As a little girl, Anna Jarvis liked to help her mother weed the flower garden in front of their home in Grafton. The garden was filled with her mother's favorite flower, the carnation.

Saddened by the division the Civil War created in many families, Anna's mother wished brothers and sisters could reunite at the side

Anna Jarvis's love for her mother prompted her to found Mother's Day.

of their mothers. Often Anna heard her mother say, "Sometime, somewhere, someone will found a Mother's day." When Mrs. Jarvis died, Anna decided to be that someone. The first Mother's Day celebration was held in Grafton on May 12, 1907. Anna said this day should "honor the best mother who ever lived—your mother."

Because of Anna Jarvis's efforts, in 1919 President Woodrow Wilson signed a proclamation declaring the second Sunday in May as Mother's Day. By the time Anna died in 1948, more than forty countries were observing Mother's Day. And because her mother loved carnations, they have become the traditional Mother's Day flower.

Cyrus Vance is another West Virginian who has made a differ-

West Virginian Cyrus Vance is a respected negotiator for peace.

U.S. senator Robert C. Byrd is one of the more colorful members of Congress. His speeches are full of homespun humor, and he plays a mean country fiddle.

ence. This former U.S. secretary of state was born in Clarksburg. In the 1960s, Vance proved himself a skilled diplomat by negotiating the release of the American ship USS *Pueblo* and its crew, which had been captured by the North Koreans. From 1991 to 1993, he served as a United Nations representative, working to resolve the conflict in Bosnia-Herzegovina, part of the former Yugoslavia.

West Virginia senator Robert C. Byrd is well known for his hard work, mastery of Senate detail, and country fiddle playing. For many years he was the Senate majority leader, the leading Democrat in the Senate. Byrd has been re-elected to the Senate five times, winning with the greatest margins of votes in West Virginia history.

Chuck Yeager, the man who broke the sound barrier, is known as the "greatest test pilot of them all."

FLYING PIONEER

Anyone interested in flying planes knows who Charles E. "Chuck" Yeager is. In 1947, Yeager became the first person to fly a jet faster than the speed of sound. Breaking the sound barrier was not what Yeager had expected: "I noticed that the faster I got, the smoother the ride. . . . I was thunderstruck. After all the anxiety, breaking the sound barrier turned out to be a perfectly paved speedway."

Born in Myra in 1923, Yeager joined the air force right out of high school. By the time he was twenty-two, he was already well known for his heroic exploits and dogfights during World War II. He eventually rose to the rank of general. Much of Yeager's life was written about in Tom Wolfe's book *The Right Stuff*. His home state honored him by naming Charleston's Yeager airport after him. Yeager's career as a test pilot opened doors for future astronauts, including Jon McBride, the first West Virginian in space.

MUSICIANS

West Virginia has a long musical tradition. The folk music of Appalachia spawned much of what is now known as country music. It is no surprise many country music stars are from West Virginia, including Grammy Award–winner Kathy Mattea. In 1990,

Grammy-winner Kathy Mattea was greatly influenced by traditional Appalachian music.

Mattea won the Grammy for Best Country Performer, and twice she has been named Female Vocalist of the Year by the Country Music Association. Mattea grew up in Cross Lanes and was influenced by the folk music she heard as a child: "I can still remember the first time I heard a hammered dulcimer. I was spellbound." Mattea now lives in Nashville, Tennessee, but she still calls West Virginia home.

Unlike Mattea, Alum Creek native Jeff Stevens made his mark as a country music songwriter. His best-known song is the George Strait hit "Carrying Your Love With Me." "Being from West Virginia has given me a huge leg up," said Stevens. "All of my family and all of my heritage and everybody I knew from there goes right into my songs."

Not all musicians from West Virginia are country. The late Don Redman was a composer, bandleader, and one of the first successful black orchestra leaders and jazz arrangers. The Piedmont native composed and arranged for big band leaders Count Basie and Jimmy Dorsey. Redman also wrote music for radio and television and was the music director for singer Pearl Bailey.

WRITERS

West Virginia's best-known writer is also one of the world's most read. Pearl S. Buck was born in Hillsboro in 1892. She won both the Nobel and Pulitzer Prizes for literature. Buck's talent lay in telling stories of ordinary people dealing with extraordinary circumstances. Her simple style made the characters seem real.

Buck lived much of her life in China, where her parents were

MOUNTAIN STAGE

Long before there was MTV's *Unplugged*, there was *Live from Mountain Stage*. Some of America's best musicians perform live before an audience at the West Virginia Cultural Center in Charleston on this weekly two-hour radio show, which is distributed worldwide by National Public Radio. "I like to think of it as one of West Virginia's best exports," says host and singer-songwriter Larry Groce.

Cajun, bluegrass, folk, Tex-Mex, blues, gospel, rock, and Celtic are some of the styles listeners can enjoy. "Musicians like it because there is not a lot of hype," says Groce. R.E.M., Kathy Mattea, Lyle Lovett, and Toad the Wet Sprocket are just a few of the musicians who have performed on the show.

Larry Groce says, "*Stage* reflects West Virginia—unpretentious, straightforward, but with a sense of humor."

Pearl S. Buck is best known for her novels about China.

missionaries. In fact, she spoke Chinese before English. Many of her novels sprang from her experiences there. Her most famous work is *The Good Earth*, but she is also known for *East Wind, West Wind*; *Dragon Seed*; and *The Living Reed*. After spending the first forty years of her life in China, Buck spent the last forty in West Virginia.

Children's author Betsy Byars was born in North Carolina in 1928. She moved to Morgantown when her husband became a professor at West Virginia University. She says one of the turning points of her career happened in 1962 when she signed up for a children's literature course at WVU. Many of her novels are set in West Virginia, including the Newberry Award–winners *The Summer of the Swans* and *Cracker Jackson*. Byars captures the spirit of childhood in her often funny books.

ATHLETES

West Virginia's most famous Olympic athlete is Mary Lou Retton. In 1984, Retton became the first U.S. gymnast to win a gold medal since 1948. Her exuberance and big smile delighted West Virginians

Champion gymnast Mary Lou Retton is famous for both her beaming smile and her fierce determination. "As the pressure gets greater, Mary Lou gets greater," said her Olympic team coach, Don Peters.

and people around the world. Retton has a street named after her in her hometown of Fairmont.

George Brett, who was born in Glen Dale in 1953, was one of baseball's greatest hitters. He won two American League batting championships with the Kansas City Royals, and in 1980 he led the Royals to the American League pennant, winning the Most Valuable Player award. In 1985, Brett had his ultimate triumph, leading the Royals to a World Series victory.

George Brett, one of baseball's best hitters, hails from Glen Dale, West Virginia.

Basketball player Jerry West was born in Cabin Creek and became an all-American player at West Virginia University. As a member of the Los Angeles Lakers, he became the first player in history to score more than four thousand playoff points. In 1981, he was named to the National Basketball Association's all-time all-star team.

It seems that no matter how far away successful West Virginians move, part of their native state stays with them. "I meet so many people from West Virginia around the country and all of them still consider themselves West Virginians—even if they've lived some-where else for twenty years," said Kathy Mattea. "It's a really significant part of who I am."

6 A TOURIST'S DREAM

It has been a long time coming, but people are finally recognizing how wonderful the Mountain State is to visit. West Virginia is a place to go rock climbing, white-water rafting, kayaking, hiking, or skiing. It is also a place to just relax and enjoy the beauty of the Appalachians.

Many people have discovered the state since the completion of major highways has made it more accessible. But to really see West Virginia, you need to get off the main highways and onto winding mountain roads.

THE SOUTH

Southern West Virginia used to be a collection of poor coal mining villages tucked away in mountain hollows. Today it looks very different.

On the north side of Beckley, a spiked, bright red roof stands out against the landscape. This is Tamarack, which is known as the Best of West Virginia. In creating Tamarack, former governor W. Gaston Caperton III envisioned a home for the state's rich cultural heritage. It is a place where jobs, marketing, training, and educational opportunities abound for West Virginia's artists, producers, craftspeople, and farmers. "West Virginia Made" textiles, glass, pottery, jewelry, baskets, specialty foods, and souvenirs are for sale

Tamarack helps West Virginia's many artists and craftspeople market their wares.

at Tamarack. The center also features five craft demonstration studios, a theater presenting films and live performances, gallery exhibits, gardens, and a nature trail.

The West Virginia state park system is one of the most beautiful in the country. Many of its best parks are located along the New River gorge. In spring, the area is bursting with rhododendron and mountain laurel blooms. Hawks Nest and Grandview State Parks both have spectacular views of the gorge.

BRIDGE DAY

"Elvis has left the bridge!" cried the crowd when twenty-nine-year-old Patrick Weldon parachuted off the New River Gorge Bridge dressed in a sequined costume reminiscent of the King of Rock and Roll, Elvis Presley.

Daredevil stunts are just part of Bridge Day, West Virginia's largest one-day festival. Celebrated on the third Saturday in October, the festival commemorates the completion of the New River Gorge Bridge in 1977. The bridge has the world's longest single-arch steel span and, at 876 feet above the New River, is the second-highest bridge in the country.

"Thank you, West Virginia!" screamed Chris Stokely of Houston, Texas, as he dove over the bridge railing. Parachutists and BASE jumpers (BASE stands for Building, Antenna, Span, Earth—the fixed objects from which these jumpers leap) love West Virginia because the New River Gorge Bridge is one of the few places in the world where they can make a lawful jump.

Beneath the bridge dangle expert rappellers, people using ropes to descend from the bridge. Resembling spiders weaving a web, they practice their well-honed skills with the breathtaking gorge as a backdrop. Other rappellers are on hand for rescue operations in the gorge if necessary. Three people have been killed since the first Bridge Day in 1980.

In 1996, four hundred parachutists and nineteen rappel teams from fifteen states and Canada attended the event. But most people come to Bridge Day just to walk across the 3,030-foot-long bridge. On this one day, the bridge is closed to traffic and open to pedestrians.

The New River itself attracts many tourists. Abandoned coal mining towns, scenic waterfalls, and tall tales told by guides are usually part of a good rafting or canoeing trip.

The once thriving railroad and mining town of Thurmond can be seen from the New River. Thurmond has a history like a Wild West town, but its population has dwindled to only a few houses hugging a gorge known as the Grand Canyon of the East. Thurmond's main street isn't a street at all. Instead, it is railroad tracks running

Springtime visitors to Grandview-Beckley State Park can delight in the blooming rhododendrons as well as the stunning view of the New River gorge.

parallel to the river, a vivid reminder of what made this community boom and then go bust. The historic Thurmond Depot has been restored and now serves as a park visitor center. Exhibits and period furnishings bring the golden days of railroading back to life. Visitors today no longer visit Thurmond for the wild times at the notorious DunGlen Hotel. Instead, many are mountain bikers just passing through.

At Babcock State Park, a mountain trout stream called Glade Creek rushes through a rocky canyon creating waterfalls as it goes. The Glade Creek Grist Mill has become a favorite with many of the nation's photographers. Reconstructed from portions of old mills from throughout the state, this fully operating mill offers freshly ground cornmeal, buckwheat, and whole wheat flour to park guests.

Bramwell is near the state's southern border with Virginia. Settled by wealthy coal mine owners at the end of the nineteenth century, Bramwell was once dubbed "the richest small town in America." It was home to as many as nineteen millionaires, who made their fortunes in the Pocahontas County coalfields. The prosperous Bank of Bramwell was the hub of southern West Virginia's financial network. The bank closed in 1933 in the midst of the Great Depression, and most of Bramwell's wealthy residents left. Today, Bramwell's former Victorian charm has been restored to delight tourists. Some of the old estates have been turned into bed and breakfast inns, and most are part of a tour highlighting the town's heyday.

The Glade Creek Grist Mill is a beautiful spot to buy some flour.

At least one southern West Virginia spot has maintained its prosperity and grandeur and still frequently welcomes famous visitors. The Greenbrier Hotel at White Sulphur Springs is one of the last grand old hotels left in the United States and is the only hotel in the nation employing a full-time historian. Robert Conte keeps the hotel's long and wonderful history alive. "I think everybody can see, they don't build them like this anymore," says Conte.

The Greenbrier has experienced much of the nation's history. During the Civil War, both Union and Confederate troops occupied the hotel. At the beginning of World War II it was used as an internment center for German and Japanese diplomats who were waiting to be traded for American diplomats abroad. "We treated their diplomats as well as possible, in hopes that Japan and Germany would do the same with ours," said Conte. Then, in September 1942, the hotel was turned into a hospital by the United States Army.

The recent revelation of one of the worst-kept secrets in the state has added to the hotel's colorful history. The Greenbrier was the sight of a top-secret bunker designed to house the members of the U.S. Congress in the event of nuclear war. The facility was built under the hotel between 1958 and 1961. The secrecy of the bunker was maintained for more than thirty years, but on May 31, 1992, the *Washington Post* published a story exposing it. The next day, the facility began to be phased out. Tours of the bunker are very popular.

THE STATE CAPITAL

West Virginia's largest city is its capital, Charleston. At the center

PLACES TO SEE

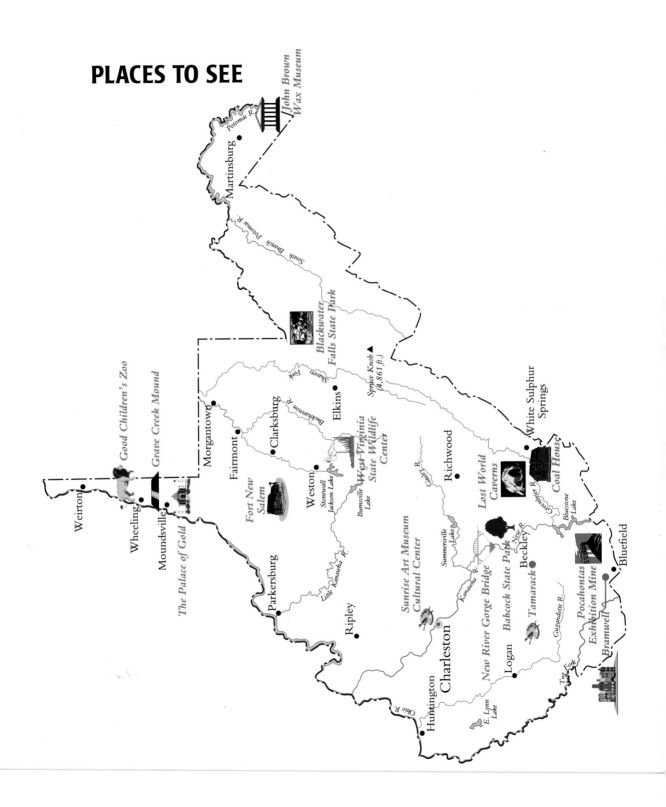

John Brown
Wax Museum

Potomac R.

Martinsburg

South Branch Potomac R.

Blackwater
Falls State Park

Shavers Fork

Spruce Knob ▲
(4,861 ft.)

White Sulphur
Springs

Good Children's Zoo

Grave Creek Mound

Morgantown

Fairmont

Clarksburg

Buckhannon R.

Elkins

West Virginia
State Wildlife
Center

Richwood

Lost World
Caverns

Coal House

Weirton

Wheeling

Moundsville

The Palace of Gold

Fort New
Salem

Weston

Stonewall
Jackson Lake

Burnsville
Lake

Gauley R.

Greenbrier R.

Bluestone
Lake

Bluefield

Parkersburg

Little Kanawha R.

Sunrise Art Museum
Cultural Center

Summersville
Lake

Kanawha R.

New River Gorge Bridge

New R.

Babcock State Park

Beckley

Tamarack

Guyandotte R.

Pocahontas
Exhibition Mine

Bramwell

Ripley

Charleston

Logan

Huntington

E. Lynn
Lake

Ohio R.

Tug Fork

of town, covered in gold leaf, shines the dome of the capitol. Completed in 1932, the building was designed by Cass Gilbert, a renowned architect who also created the Supreme Court building in Washington, D.C., and the capitols of Minnesota and Arkansas. The dome of West Virginia's capitol is 292 feet high, higher than the dome on the nation's capitol in Washington.

Also on the capitol grounds is the State Museum, which has displays illustrating life in the Mountain State from its Indian past to the present. Charleston is also the site of the Sunrise Museum, which has art and science exhibits, a planetarium, and a children's museum.

Each May, Charleston hosts the Vandalia Gathering, a celebration of traditional Appalachian music. Visitors listen to the sweet sounds of fiddles, banjos, and mountain dulcimers. The city's best-known festival comes in September, when every boat around seems to be out on the Kanawha for Charleston's regatta. Craft booths and food courts line the riverbanks, and both land and river lovers delight in a spectacular fireworks display.

THE NORTHERN PANHANDLE

South of Wheeling is Moundsville and the Grave Creek Mound State Park, where modern American archaeology was born. In 1881, Congress gave the Smithsonian Institution five thousand dollars for the excavation and study of Native American burial mounds. The first excavation was of the Grave Creek Mound, one of the most famous and certainly the largest of the Adena Indian burial mounds. Constructed between 250 to 150 B.C., the mound is 69 feet high and 295 feet across and contains over 60,000 tons of earth. Excavation of these mounds has unearthed artifacts like a copper headdress and flint knives. By the time the Smithsonian completed its excavation project in 1890, over two thousand mounds and earthworks had been studied in the eastern United States. About a hundred of these were in the Kanawha Valley.

The best place to enjoy Charleston's regatta is in a boat floating down the Kanawha River.

THE EASTERN PANHANDLE

Only about an hour's drive away from the nation's capital, the eastern panhandle has become part of Washington, D.C.'s suburban outskirts. Despite growing urbanization, the area has maintained its natural beauty and early American charm.

Historical sights are scattered throughout the eastern panhandle. Long before the first Europeans discovered its warm waters, Berkeley Springs was already a famous health spa attracting Native Americans from Canada to the Carolinas. The springs became a favorite of George Washington as early as 1748, but not until 1756 did North America's first public mineral springs resort open there. Heat and pressure deep below the earth's surface cause the springwater to gush out of the ground at a soothing 74 degrees Fahrenheit.

PEAK OF THE ALLEGHENIES

The stretch of the Alleghenies at the base of the eastern panhandle resembles Canada more than the southern United States. In winter, Spruce Knob, West Virginia's highest point, and is often unreachable because of the ice and snow. In spring and summer, mountain bikers and hikers work hard to get to the top. Those who make it are rewarded with a spectacular view. As you climb the peak, the thick pine forests give way to more barren, rocky terrain. On top, most trees only have branches on one side because cold winds freeze growth on the other. At Spruce Knob's peak, miles of green valleys and rising forests can be seen. Eagles and hawks often soar over the landscape. It is a good place just to sit quietly. "You realize how small a part of the universe you are from up here," said one hiker.

Southwest of Spruce Knob is Seneca Rocks, a sandstone rock formation that looks out of place among the surrounding forested ridges. Bare and dramatic in its form, it resembles parts of the southwestern United States. Serious rock climbers test their skills on the nine-hundred-foot cliff there.

Seneca Rocks remain a favorite among serious rock climbers.

The bog at Dolly Sods is sometimes a sea of blooms.

Some visitors return again and again to view the stunning Blackwater Falls.

Seneca Rocks seem to spring up out of nowhere.

THE NATIONAL RADIO ASTRONOMY OBSERVATORY

Sometimes you can learn as much from listening as from seeing. By listening for sounds in space, the telescopes at the National Radio Astronomy Observatory in Deer Creek valley can tell scientists all sorts of things about the universe. They can help answer questions concerning what space is made of, the nature of time, and whether other stars and galaxies exist that we do not know about.

To most people, radio waves just sound like a lot of static. But scientists armed with computers can tell much from what they hear. A change in rhythm or pitch can indicate the location of a planet, moon, or other object in space.

Radio telescopes look like huge satellite dishes. The observatory's newest machine, the Green Bank Telescope, is the largest steerable telescope in the world.

The National Radio Astronomy Observatory is located in rural West Virginia for good reason. The remoteness of Deer Creek valley and the surrounding mountains protect the sensitive receivers used on the telescopes against unwanted radio interference.

At Dolly Sods, trails lead hikers through arctic bogs. But visitors must read warning signs and be careful where they walk. During World War II, Dolly Sods was used for military exercises, and some live mortar shells are buried in the soil. The forest service continues to clear the area of these hidden hazards, but some shells are still out there. If a hiker happens upon an unexploded shell, they are warned, *do not touch it*. While discovering shells is extremely rare, they are occasionally found by hunters and backcountry hikers.

At Blackwater Falls State Park, the six-story-high falls can be seen from several vantage points at the edge of the Blackwater River gorge. They are a spectacular sight for both first-time visitors and devout fans of this park.

Beautiful scenery and train and logging industry history are all part of a trip on the Cass Scenic Railroad. The route takes riders from the old lumber town of Cass to the summit of Bald Knob, the second-highest peak in the state. The train is powered by a specially designed Shay steam locomotive, which was once used to haul logs. Now it takes passengers past breathtaking mountain scenery. The railroad is the last remaining segment of the massive lumber railroad network that once covered every valley and mountain in Pocahontas County. The sawmills that these railroads supplied with timber made Pocahontas County one of the leading lumber-producing areas in the eastern United States for many years.

Full of history and natural beauty, a sportsman's paradise and a quiet retreat, West Virginia is truly wild and wonderful. It is a place visitors are happy to find and natives love to return to.

THE FLAG: Adopted in 1929, the state flag features the state seal against a white background with a blue border. At the top of the seal are the words "State of West Virginia." Rhododendrons, the state flower, surround the rest of the seal.

THE SEAL: Adopted in 1863, the state seal bears the words "State of West Virginia" and the state motto "Montani Semper Liberi" (Mountaineers Are Always Free). In the center, a farmer and a miner stand next to a rock with the date 1863, the year West Virginia became a state. In front of the rock are two rifles, which symbolize willingness to fight for freedom.

STATE SURVEY

Statehood: June 20, 1863

Origin of Name: Western counties of the state of Virginia separated from the state during the Civil War rather than secede from the Union. Virginia was named for Elizabeth I, the Virgin Queen of England.

Nickname: Mountain State, Panhandle State

Capital: Charleston

Motto: *Montani Semper Liberi* (Mountaineers Are Always Free)

Bird: Cardinal

Animal: Black bear

Fish: Brook trout

Flower: Rhododendron

Tree: Sugar maple

Insect: Monarch butterfly

Fruit: Golden Delicious apple

Colors: Gold and blue

Cardinal

Black bear

THE WEST VIRGINIA HILLS

West Virginia has three state songs, but in 1961 the state legislature stated in an official resolution that this was the best known and most widely sung in the state. The words were written in 1879 and set to music in 1885.

Words by Rev. David King

Music by H. E. Engle

GEOGRAPHY

Highest point: 4,865 feet above sea level at Spruce Knob

Lowest point: 240 feet above sea level along the Potomac River in Harpers Ferry

Area: 24,231 square miles

Greatest Distance, North to South: 237 miles

Greatest Distance, East to West: 265 miles

Bordering States: Ohio to the northwest, Pennsylvania and Maryland to the north, Virginia to the east and south, Kentucky to the southwest

Hottest Recorded Temperature: 112°F at Martinsburg on July 10, 1936, and at Moorefield on August 4, 1930

Coldest Recorded Temperature: -37°F at Lewisburg on December 30, 1917

Average Annual Precipitation: 44 inches

Major Rivers: Guyandotte, Kanawha, Little Kanawha, Monongahela, New, Ohio, Potomac, Tygart, West Fork

Major Lakes: There are no large natural lakes; artificial reservoirs have been created on the New, Gauley, and Tygart Rivers

Trees: beech, cherry, hemlock, hickory, maple, oak, poplar, red spruce, white pine

Hickory

Wild Plants: aster, azalea, black-eyed Susan, bloodroot, dogwood, golden-rod, hepatica, redbud, rhododendron, white-blossomed hawthorn, wild crab apple

Animals: black bear, bobcat, gray fox, groundhog, mink, opossum, otter, rabbit, raccoon, red fox, skunk, squirrel, white-tailed deer

Fish: bass, bluegill, crappie, muskellunge, pickerel, trout, walleyed pike

Birds: brown thrasher, cardinal, eagle, falcon, hawk, quail, scarlet tanager, snipe, wood thrush

Endangered Animals: American peregrine falcon, bald eagle, Cheat mountain salamander, fanshell, flat-spired three-toothed snail, harperella, Indiana bat, James River spinymussel, northeastern bulrush, northern riffleshell, pink mucket pearlymussel, Virginia big-eared bat, Virginia northern flying squirrel

Flying squirrel

Endangered Plants: running buffalo clover, Virginia spiraea

TIMELINE

West Virginia History

c. 1000 B.C. The mound-building Adena Indians inhabit the area

A.D. 1600s Iroqouis Confederacy tribes hunt in the region

1669 John Lederer, the first European to see western Virginia, travels to the top of the Blue Ridge

1671 Englishmen Thomas Batts and Robert Fallam cross the Allegheny Mountains, which helps England claim the Ohio Valley

1742 John P. Salling and John Howard discover coal on the Coal River

1754–1755 Frenchmen and Indians defeat British troops led by George Washington and General Edward Braddock during the French and Indian War

1773 Plans for a 14th colony, which would include West Virginia, collapse

1782 Although the American Revolution has ended, British troops and Indians raid Fort Henry at Wheeling

1788 Charleston is founded

1788 Daniel Boone settles in Kanawha Valley

1815 Natural gas is discovered near Charleston

1836 B&O (Baltimore and Ohio) Railroad from Chesapeake Bay reaches Harpers Ferry

1859 John Brown raids the federal arsenal at Harpers Ferry

1861 Western counties of Virginia refuse to secede from the Union; they form their own government, the Restored Government of Virginia

1863 West Virginia becomes the 35th state

1872 State constitution is ratified

1890 United Mine Workers of America (UMWA) begin to organize in the state

1907 Worst mining disaster in U.S. history leaves 361 dead at Monongah

1919–1921 Labor disputes involving coal miners break out in Logan and Mingo Counties

1924 West Virginian John W. Davis becomes Democratic presidential nominee but loses to Calvin Coolidge

1954 The West Virginia Turnpike opens

1959 National Radio Astronomy Observatory begins operating at Green Bank

1968 Explosions and fire in a coal mine in Farmington kill 78 people and lead to new mining safety laws

1972 Buffalo Creek flood kills more than 100 people near Man

1985 State lottery is established

ECONOMY

Agricultural Products: apples, corn, hay, livestock and livestock products (beef, chicken, milk, turkeys), peaches, tobacco

Manufactured Products: chemicals, food products, glass products, machinery, pottery, steel

Natural Resources: clay, coal, gravel, limestone, natural gas, petroleum, rock salt, sand

Business and Trade: communication, tourism, transportation

CALENDAR OF CELEBRATIONS

Feast of the Ramson In April, Richwood and other towns celebrate the ramp, a wild leek that grows between April and June. The Richwood festival features an old-fashioned ramp dinner, as well as arts and crafts, old-time music, and dancing. At the Elkins ramp celebration, you can eat ramps fried, boiled, and any other way you can think of at the Ramp Cook-Off.

Blue and Gray Reunion During the first weekend of June in Philippi, actors re-create the first land battle of the Civil War. Other events during this living history weekend include artillery demonstrations and a costumed Civil War ball.

Sternwheel Regatta and River Festival At this June festival in Point Pleasant,

you can enjoy sternwheel races, towboat demonstrations, a parade, dancing, and arts-and-crafts displays.

West Virginia State Fair This nine-day fair in Lewisburg in early August draws exhibitors and visitors from throughout the region. Enjoy horse shows, food, livestock competitions, and musical entertainment.

West Virginia Oil and Gas Festival In early September, Sisterville celebrates its history as an oil boomtown with a parade, a gas-engine show, a wood-chopping contest, an antique car show, a crafts fair, oil and gas equipment displays, and a fiddling contest.

Civil War Days During the second week of September, Gauley Bridge, the site of heavy fighting during the Civil War, honors its past. You can watch a Civil War re-enactment staged at Carnifax Ferry Battlefield State Park and also enjoy parades, sporting events, and wood-chopping contests.

Country Roads Festival During the third week of September, visitors to

Hawks Nest State Park in Ansted kick up their heels with great bluegrass and gospel music, and clogging, a form of dancing.

Mountaineer Balloon Festival Fall in Morgantown brings this three-day celebration of flight. Watch the launch of dozens of colorful hot-air balloons and then enjoy music and carnival rides.

West Virginia Italian Heritage Festival This September celebration in Clarksburg honors the state's citizens of Italian descent. Costumed minstrels, singers, dancers, actors, and puppeteers entertain visitors.

Mountain State Forest Festival Highlights of the state's oldest festival, held in Elkins in October, include wood-chopping contests, parades, and jousting. The festival also features crafts, food, and the crowning of the festival's Queen Silvia.

Battle Days For two days in October, Point Pleasant remembers the 1774 battle that some historians call the opening exchange of the Revolutionary War. The celebration includes military re-enactments, a colonial ball with period costumes, music and dance, a parade, and an ox roast.

Apple Butter Festival If it's Columbus Day weekend, it's time to savor the apple butter at Berkeley Springs. You can also enjoy the music and crafts, but the emphasis is on food—especially the apple butter simmering in giant kettles over open fires.

Old Tyme Christmas A candlelit walk, caroling, and children's programs during the first two weekends in December help visitors to Harpers Ferry get into the holiday spirit.

STATE STARS

Nnamdi Azikiwe (1904–1996) was the first president of the Republic of Nigeria. He attended Storer College in Harpers Ferry.

Nnamdi Azikiwe

Randy Barnes (1966–   ), born in Charleston, won a gold medal in the shot put at the 1996 Olympics in Atlanta. He also holds the world record in shot put.

Randy Barnes

Pearl Buck (1892–1973), born in Hillsboro, was the third American to receive the Nobel Prize for literature. She was the daughter of American missionaries and lived in China until 1933. She returned to the United

States and lived the rest of her life in West Virginia. She is best known for her novels set in China, especially *The Good Earth*, for which she won a Pulitzer Prize in 1932.

Robert C. Byrd (1917–) was born in North Carolina but was raised by relatives in West Virginia after his mother died. Byrd has been a leading Democrat in the U.S. Senate since 1959. Byrd entered politics in 1946, serving in the West Virginia House of Delegates, the state senate, and the U.S. House of Representatives, before being elected to the U.S. Senate. He is well known for his mastery of the complex legislative system.

Stephen Coonts (1946–), author of the Vietnam War novel *Flight of the Intruder*, was born in Morgantown. He also wrote the best-sellers *The Cannibal Queen*, *Final Flight*, *The Minotaur*, *Under Siege*, and *The Red Horseman*.

George Henry Crumb (1929–), born in Charleston, is a composer known for his innovative use of instrumental and vocal effects, such as hissing, whispering, tongue-clicking, and shouting. His most famous work is *Echoes of Time and the River*, which earned him a Pulitzer Prize in music in 1968.

John W. Davis (1873–1955) was the Democratic candidate for president in 1924, but he lost to Calvin Coolidge. Prior to this, Davis had served in the U.S. House of Representatives and as the U.S. ambassador to Great Britain. He was also solicitor general in Woodrow Wilson's administration and argued more cases before the

John W. Davis

Supreme Court than any other attorney in history. Davis was born in Clarksburg.

Thomas "Stonewall" Jackson (1824–1863), a leading Confederate general in the Civil War, was born in Clarksburg. He earned his nickname at the First Battle of Bull Run in 1861, when his troops stood "like a stone wall" against the Union army. His soldiers defeated Union forces in 1862 in the Shenandoah Valley. He then joined Robert E. Lee's campaign to drive Union troops from Richmond. He also took part in Southern victories at Antietam and Fredericksburg. He was wounded at the battle of Chancellorsville in 1863 by his own troops, who had mistaken him for an enemy. He died from his wounds.

Thomas "Stonewall" Jackson

Anna M. Jarvis (1864–1948), the founder of Mother's Day, was born near Grafton. After the death of her mother in 1907, she began campaigning to have a day set aside honoring mothers. The first Mother's Day was celebrated in Grafton on May 12, 1907. In 1915, President Woodrow Wilson proclaimed the second Sunday of each May as Mother's Day.

Don Knotts (1924–   ), television and movie actor, was born in Morgantown, the son of farmers. He attended West Virginia University. Knotts is best known for his role on the *Andy Griffith Show* as Deputy Barney Fife.

John Knowles (1926–   ), born in Fairmont, is the author of the novel

A Separate Peace, which tells the story of two friends at a New England prep school during World War II.

Kathy Mattea (1959–   ), born in South Charleston, is a successful country singer. In 1990, she won a Grammy as Best Country Performer. Twice she has been named Female Vocalist of the Year by the Country Music Association.

George Armitage Miller (1920–   ) is a psychologist whose studies of language were pioneering works in psycholinguistics. From 1960 to 1967 he was the director of Harvard University's Center for Cognitive Studies. He is the author of many works on psychology, including *Language and Speech*. He was born in Charleston.

Francis H. Pierpont (1814–1899) born near Morgantown, is known as the father of West Virginia. When Virginia seceded from the Union, Pierpont organized people loyal to the North in the western part of the state. At the Wheeling Convention he was named governor of the Restored State of Virginia, the seceding western Virginia area.

Mary Lou Retton (1968–   ), 1984 Olympic gold medal gymnast, was born in Fairmont. She began gymnastics lessons at age 7 and moved to Houston, Texas, at age 14 to train with Romanian coach Bela Karolyi. At age 16, she became the first American ever to win an individual all-around gold medal in gymnastics. She also won two silver medals (vault and team competition) and two bronze medals (floor exercise and parallel bars). Her exuberant smile and spirit made her a popular athlete and put her on the front of the Wheaties box.

Walter Reuther (1907–1970), born in Wheeling, was president of the Unit-

Walter Reuther

ed Automobile Workers union from 1946 until his death. He was also president of the Congress of Industrial Organizations (CIO) from 1952 to 1955. He engineered the merger of the American Federation of Labor (AFL) and CIO in 1955 and served as vice president of the AFL-CIO between 1955 and 1968. Reuther had started working in a factory at age 16 and soon became involved in union causes. During his career, Reuther won annual wage increases based on productivity, cost-of-living raises, and health and pension benefits for his union members.

James Rumsey (1743–1792) is often called the inventor of the steamboat. He demonstrated a steamboat on the Potomac at Shepherdstown in 1787. Rumsey died before his second demonstration model was finished.

Soupy Sales (1926–   ), a radio and television comedian, grew up in Huntington with the name Milton Hines. He is called the world's leading authority on pie-throwing, a trademark of his comedy act. Sales hosted his own TV show from 1953 to 1960.

Soupy Sales

Harry Ford Sinclair (1876–1956), born in Wheeling, founded Sinclair Oil, which later became Atlantic Richfield, one of the world's largest oil companies. Sinclair gained notoriety during the 1920s, when he was charged with bribery and conspiracy to defraud the government during the so-called Teapot Dome oil field scandal that rocked the Warren G. Harding presidency. He was acquitted.

Harry Ford Sinclair

Cyrus Vance (1917–   ) was U.S. secretary of state from 1977 to 1980 while Jimmy Carter was president. He also served as secretary of the army, deputy secretary of defense, and as a U.S. delegate during the Paris peace conference on Vietnam. As secretary of state he was involved in the Strategic Arms Limitation Talks, the negotiations leading to the Israeli-Egyptian peace treaty of 1979, and the efforts to secure release of U.S. hostages in Iran. Vance was born in Clarksburg.

Booker T. Washington (1856–1915) was a highly respected educator and a black leader. The son of slaves, Washington was born in Franklin County, Virginia, and moved to Malden, West Virginia, with his family after the Civil War. In 1881, he became the first president of Tuskegee Institute, an Alabama trade school for blacks. Under his leadership, the school became a major agricultural and industrial college for African Americans. Washington believed that blacks needed an education if they were to win equality and integration. He became a well-known public speaker and advised Presidents Theodore Roosevelt and William Howard Taft on racial matters. *Up From Slavery* is Washington's well-known autobiography.

Booker T. Washington

Jerry West (1938–   ), born in Cheylan, is considered one of the greatest basketball players ever. In 14 years with the Los Angeles Lakers, he played on 13 consecutive all-star teams. In the 1969–70 season he led the National Basketball Association in scoring with a 31.2 point average. Two years later, he led the league in assists with 747. When he retired in 1974, he ranked third in regular-season career scoring, with 25,192 points and had a career average of 27 points per game. He later served as coach and general manager of the Lakers.

Jerry West

Chuck Yeager (1923–   ) was the first person to travel faster than the speed of sound. Born in Myra, he enlisted in the army in 1941 and became an air force pilot in 1943. During World War II, he flew 64 missions and shot down 13 German aircraft. After the war, he became a test pilot and in 1947, he broke the sound barrier of 662 mph. In 1953, Yeager set a speed record of 1,650 mph. He wrote two books, *Yeager* and *Press On.*

TOUR THE STATE

Beckley Exhibition Coal Mine (Beckley) Real coal miners guide visitors in remodeled mine cars through 1,500 feet of underground passageways in this former coal mine. A coal company house depicts the difficult life of a coal miner's family. You can also visit the mine museum and stay overnight in the campground nearby.

Theatre West Virginia (Beckley) At the Cliffside Amphitheater in Grandview State Park, this theater company presents two musicals: *The Hatfields and McCoys* about the Hatfield-McCoy feud and *Honey in the Rock* about the formation of the state.

Youth Museum of Southern West Virginia (Beckley) Experience the state's history at the heritage center, which features a mountain homestead, a one-room schoolhouse, a blacksmith shop, a loom room, and a frontier garden. You can also learn about the night skies at the planetarium and get a glimpse of 1880s railroad life through a collection of wood carvings.

State Capitol Complex (Charleston) The outstanding feature of the capitol is its gold-leaf rotunda, which is five feet higher than that of the

New River Gorge Bridge

U.S. Capitol's dome. From the center of the 292-foot-high gold dome hangs a rock crystal chandelier weighing two tons. Also in the complex are the governor's mansion, the Booker T. Washington Memorial, and the State Museum, which traces state history from Indian migration to the early 20th century. Highlights include a settler's cabin, a general store, and Civil War exhibits.

South Charleston Mound (South Charleston) This Adena Indian mound was built as a burial site for chieftains during the first century A.D. It is the second-largest mound in the state, measuring 175 feet in diameter by 35 feet high.

Museum of Radio and Technology (Huntington) At this museum, you can listen to recordings of old radio shows, tour exhibits of the history of radio, and trace the development of broadcasting from radio to television to video.

Pilgrim Glass Corporation (Huntington) Watch glassmaking at one of the world's largest manufacturers of cranberry, cobalt, and crystal glass.

West Virginia State Farm Museum (Point Pleasant) This 50-acre museum features 31 reconstructed buildings, including log cabins built in the early 1800s, a replica of an old Lutheran church, a one-room schoolhouse, a print shop, a doctor's office, a country store, a blacksmith shop, an herb garden, railroad cars, and farm equipment.

Grave Creek Mound State Park (Moundsville) This is the largest conical prehistoric burial mound of its kind. It measures 69 feet high and 295 feet in diameter. The Grave Creek Mound was built more than 2,000 years ago by the Adena Indians. The nearby Delf Norona Museum and Cultural Center displays Indian artifacts from 1000 B.C. to A.D. 1.

The Palace of Gold (Moundsville) This palace was dubbed America's Taj Mahal by the *New York Times* because of its elaborate rooms which are decorated with more than 40 varieties of imported marble and onyx. The grounds also include the Imperial Elephant Restaurant and the Court of Roses gardens.

Oglebay Park (Wheeling) This park contains gardens, greenhouses, and a glass museum. A computerized light-and-sound show on Schenk Lake dazzles visitors. An 1863 train tours the Good Children's Zoo where you can see more than 200 North American animal species.

Independence Hall (Wheeling) If you're a Civil War buff, you'll want to visit the former capitol of the Restored Government of Virginia, now a museum and part of the Civil War Discovery Trail. Independence Hall once served as a customhouse, a post office, and a federal court and was the site of the Second Wheeling Convention where the state's Declaration of Independence was written.

West Virginia Penitentiary (Wheeling) Walk through the first territorial prison in the state and experience the dreary Alamo Cell Block where the worst of the inmates spent 22 hours a day. Murals painted by inmates decorate the walls.

Pricketts Fort State Park (Fairmont) At this park, you can learn about 18th-century life in West Virginia from costumed guides and craftspeople. The reconstructed fort is similar to one built on the same site in 1774. The amphitheater features presentations about the pioneers who settled the area.

Jackson's Mill Museum (Weston) This museum is located on the original five-acre site of Stonewall Jackson's boyhood home. An old mill, blacksmithing equipment, carpentry tools, and weaving equipment are on display. Two furnished 18th-century log cabins are also on the grounds.

Berkeley Castle (Berkeley Springs) This half-scale copy of Lord William Berkeley's castle in England was built in 1885. (Berkeley was the third colonial governor of Virginia.) Called by some a Victorian folly, the castle features a large stone-walled ballroom, a wide carved staircase, a tower room, and an antiques collection.

James Rumsey Historical Monument and Museum (Shepherdstown) A park and monument mark the site on the Potomac where James

Rumsey launched the first steamboat in 1787. The museum houses a half-size working replica of that boat.

Gerrard House (Gerrardstown) Built in 1743, this is one of the oldest-known buildings in West Virginia. A ladder and trapdoor provide access to the second floor of this two-story stone house.

Harpers Ferry National Historical Park (Harpers Ferry) The highlights of this 2,300-acre park are the six Paths through History: Industry, John Brown, Civil War, African-American History, Environmental History, and Transportation. Other attractions include the Industry Museum, the Wetlands Museum, John Brown's Fort, the Black Voices Museum, the Civil War Museum, and Jefferson Rock.

Blackwater Falls State Park (Davis) You can enjoy hiking, riding, picnicking, nature programs, and other outdoor activities at this lovely park, but most people come to view the 65-feet-high Blackwater Falls.

Smoke Hole Caverns (Petersburg) This underground world contains one of the world's longest ribbon stalactites, a lake, and a stream. The caverns were used by American Indians to smoke meat and by settlers to make moonshine. They were also used to store ammunition during the Civil War.

Cass Scenic Railroad (Cass) Take a ride on an old steam locomotive past mountain views to the top of Bald Knob, the second-highest peak in the state. You will pass through Cass, which was a large lumbering community at the beginning of the 20th century and is now one of the best-preserved lumber company towns in the country.

Lost World Caverns (Lewisburg) Here you can explore large rooms below the earth and marvel at the stalagmite, stalactite, and flowstone formations. One formation is more than 40 feet high and 25 feet around. The main cavern at Lost World is 1,000 feet long and nearly 75 feet wide.

North House Museum (Lewisburg) This restored home from 1820 is noted for its fine architectural detail, such as elaborate hand-carved woodwork. Now a museum, it displays military and civilian items from the Revolutionary and Civil War periods, including a covered wagon.

President's Cottage (White Sulphur Springs) This was the first private cottage built at the Greenbrier Hotel, a historic spa founded at the sulphur springs discovered in 1778. This cottage was named President's Cottage because five pre–Civil War presidents vacationed at the spa. In 1932, the cottage became a museum of the Greenbrier's colorful history.

FUN FACTS

Can you name West Virgina's oldest town? Both Shepherdstown and Romney claim the honor. Shepherdstown was originally established by Thomas Shepherd, who laid out 50 acres of his land into lots and streets. He then asked the Virginia House of Burgesses for a bill of incorporation. He filed his bill six days before a bill was filed for Romney. Both bills were signed the same day in 1762, but Romney's bill was signed first. So, technically, Romney is the oldest town.

It took 24 years to complete the B&O Railroad between Baltimore, Maryland, and the Ohio River. Two crews, one working west from Baltimore and one working east from Wheeling, met in the Grave Creek Valley, 18 miles east of Wheeling on Christmas Eve, 1852. At the time, the B&O

was the longest railroad in the world, and it was probably the most difficult to build—it had to pass through the rugged Allegheny Mountains.

The girl pictured on the Sunmaid raisins box is Lorraine Collett Petersen
of West Virginia. She was sent to San Francisco's Panama-Pacific Exposi-
tion in 1915 to pass out raisin samples. A Sunmaid executive noticed her
red bonnet among all the blue bonnets the other girls were wearing and
invited her to pose for the famous company trademark.

FIND OUT MORE

If you want to find out more about West Virginia, look in your local library or bookstore for the following titles:

GENERAL STATE BOOKS

DiPiazza, Domenica. *Hello U.S.A.: West Virginia*. Minneapolis: Lerner, 1995.

Fradin, Dennis. *From Sea to Shining Sea: West Virginia*. Chicago: Children's Press, 1994.

Stein, Conrad. *America the Beautiful: West Virginia*. Chicago: Children's Press, 1991.

SPECIAL INTEREST BOOKS

Barrett, Tracy. *Harpers Ferry: The Story of John Brown's Raid*. Brookfield, CT: Millbrook Press, 1995.

Phelan, Mary Kay. *Mother's Day*. New York: Thomas Y. Crowell Company, 1965.

FICTION

Byars, Betsy. *Summer of the Swans*. New York: Viking, 1970.

Byars, Betsy. *Cracker Jackson*. New York: Viking Kestral, 1985.

Patterson, Katherine. *Bridge to Terabithia*. New York: HarperCollins, 1977.

INTERNET

West Virginia Home Page at www.state.wv.us

West Virginia Library Commission at www.wvlc.wvnet.edu

INDEX

Chart, graph, and illustration page numbers are in boldface.